THE WOMAN WITH TWO HEADS

THE WOMAN
WITH TWO
HEADS

Elizabeth Cody Newenhuyse

WORD PUBLISHING
Dallas · London · Vancouver · Melbourne

THE WOMAN WITH TWO HEADS:
SANITY AND ENCOURAGEMENT FOR WOMEN WHO FEEL THE TUG
OF DIVIDED LOYALTIES

Scripture quotations noted as RSV are from The Revised Standard Version, copyrighted 1946, 1952, © 1971, 1973 by the Division of Christian Education of the National Council of the Churches of Christ in the U.S.A., and are used by permission.

"Workboots," by Charlotte M. Mesimore, © 1990 IHS Studio. Used by permission.

Library of Congress Cataloging-in-Publication Data:

Newenhuyse, Elizabeth Cody.
    The woman with two heads : sanity and encouragement for women who feel the tug of divided loyalties / Elizabeth Cody Newenhuyse.
        p. cm.
    ISBN 0-8499-0868-X
    1. Working mothers — United States — Psychology.
    2. Working mothers — United States — Religious life.
    I. Title
    HQ759.48.N49 1991
    306.874'3 — dc20   91-16724
                                                        CIP

1 2 3 4 9   AGF   9 8 7 6 5 4 3 2 1

Printed in the United States of America

To my mother and the memory of my father

Contents

Acknowledgments   9
Prologue: How Do You Do It?   11
Introduction: Pretty Pictures, Real Lives   13

1. Hold On to the Morning   17
2. A Call? Is It for Me?   23
3. Always a Full-Time Mom   31
4. Can't We Just Be Friends?   39
5. Loving the Good, Living with the Bad   47
6. Have a Nice Evening   53
7. "I'll Always Be Around"   59
8. In Search of a Date Night   63
9. Man of Sorrows   73
10. Why I Said Yes to the Church Committee   79
11. I Want to Be Alone (Sometimes)   87
12. When I Grow Up I Want to Be   95
     Suzie Homemaker
13. Thank God It's Sunday   101
14. Giving My Child a Summer   109
15. But What Are You Saving Time For?   115
16. Give It to Me Leaded   123
17. Why You Can't Get It All Done, and Why   129
     It's Okay
18. Let's Keep in Touch—Really   135
19. Nesting and Soaring   143
20. Woman Flees Perfection Police   149
21. Real Men Don't Dust   157
22. My Dad's Pencil Box   163
23. November's Truth   169
24. George Bailey Was Wrong   175
25. Pretty Pictures, Real Lives   183

Introduction

Pretty Pictures, Real Lives

Cozy portrait: A woman sits in her house in the morning, sun streaming through freshly ironed curtains, as she sips coffee and studies her Bible, yellow highlighter in hand. *Reality:* A woman nags at her kindergartener to stop dawdling over her Cheerios while she tries to apply mascara, mousse her hair, and search for her briefcase—all at the same time. Her curtains are an indeterminate shade of yellow. "Mister Rogers" on the television fails to calm. Her Bible is crammed into a pile somewhere.

Cozy portrait: A busy, happy family organizes a monthly master calendar to track everyone's activities. Even though both parents and children are involved in myriad pursuits, everyone manages to be home for a homemade dinner every night. *Reality:* The phone rings during dinner. The woman scrambles to find a piece of paper to write a message on. The caller is Olan Mills. She returns to dinner, which is macaroni and cheese with tuna and canned peas.

Cozy portrait: A mother sits serenely at her sewing machine, making Halloween costumes for her children. Not only is she creating costumes, she is making memories. *Reality:* "Whaddaya mean, you don't want to be a hobo for Halloween? Here—try on this old shirt!"

Cozy portrait: A husband and wife work together preparing beef stroganoff, a crisp green salad, and

crusty warm bread for a small dinner party. Everything is spotless. *Reality:* "Hon, what's
this . . . thing in the crisper drawer? It looks like it's
starting to . . . move."
     Cozy portrait: Silk flowers . . . refinished table-
tops . . . cranberry glass . . . simmering potpourri
. . . organized silverware drawers. *Reality:* Weeds
. . . water rings . . . broken ceramic birds waiting
to be glued . . . teakettles that get thrown away
because the water boiled out of them . . . crammed
closets.
     Cozy portrait: Plenty of unhurried time.
Reality: "A whole hour to myself! Such an embarrass-
ment of riches! . . . Now—what chore is undone,
what person unattended to?"

     My life is very different from the comfy idylls
sketched above—the type of picture-perfect snapshots
so often captured in many Christian books and magazines. Sometimes that bothers me; I wrestle with the
nagging feeling that Everyone Else is in step but me. I
am just enough of a traditionalist that those idylls
have great appeal—but enough of a realist to know
that most people's lives don't look like that (and
maybe never did).
     Like so many others today, I am a working woman.
I work full time in an editorial office, part time at home as
a writer, and care for a husband, young daughter, and
small house. I work both out of calling and necessity.
Usually I try to slide through, doing the best I can. I think
I am what psychologist Kevin Leman calls a "discour-
aged perfectionist," someone who makes ambitious,
detailed lists and becomes irritated with herself because
she never completes them. I don't always get enough
sleep; I know I don't get enough exercise. I try to keep up
with friends, church, extended family, laundry (actually,

Prologue

How Do You Do It?

She is four months pregnant and already showing healthily. I can't help grinning when I see her; she
is short and looks almost as wide as she is high, like a
Hummel figurine. Even her face, apple-cheeked and
usually beaming, makes me think of some old-fashioned doll.

But she doesn't look like a Hummel figurine
today as she lowers herself into the chair in my office.
She looks serious, concerned. "I want to ask you
something," she says. "I've admired the way you
seem to balance motherhood and career. You're
obviously a good mother, but somehow you've kept
your identity. I don't know many women who seem
to be able to do that."

"How do you do it?"

She has been married eight years. This will be her
first child. Through those years she has worked full
time almost continuously, both out of choice and
necessity. She is accustomed to the organized hum of
an office, working with computers and male col-
leagues, dressing in skirts, using paper clips and
Post-Its supplied as if by magic.

All this is going to change for her. She is not
certain whether she will come back part time or work
freelance at home; she knows (and I have so urged
her) she does not want to work full time while the
baby needs her like a baby needs no one else. If she
takes the freelance option—admittedly risky—she
wants to pursue it purposefully. No dabbling at home

for her! But what if her baby's colicky? What about child care? Can she work during the infant's naps? Will she miss an office, lose out on her career? Who will she be?

Tell me, she says. How do you manage it all?

Well, of course I am flattered by her question, flattered she assumes I handle the multiple demands of my life with ease, pleased she admires my apparent self-confidence.

Then I stop and think: *Well, how do I do it? Am I doing it? What can I tell this pink-faced soon-to-be mother? She knows me too well to accept any stale chestnuts. I have to be candid.*

Am I organized? Sort of. Do I have help at home? Yes, a willing husband. Do I have a formula? Nope, never touch the stuff.

Okay, so how do I do it?

And the answer that presents itself is this: By grace and with mirrors. That's how I do it.

my husband has taken over that one—even though he's unclear on the concepts of sorting and folding). I pray on the wing and think a lot about God's will for my life.

Some days I am torn: When I'm at work, I wonder how my daughter's getting along. When I'm at home, I become restless and worry about an unfinished writing project. Sometimes I feel like the woman with two heads!

And yet one day, as I was out walking with my daughter, I started to think about ways I could achieve a perfectly balanced life. *Should I give up my career and devote myself to my family?* I wondered. *But even if we could afford it — which we can't — would I want to quit working?*

Then it came to me in one of those revelatory, electric insights that feels like truth: I may never resolve this conflict. I may just have to live with it— even embrace it.

Here, then, is the paradox. I have too many things I love! And they keep bumping into each other. My life is overpopulated with positive choice. If I choose one option—spending time with my child—I have less to give my career. If I decide to concentrate on my work, I risk neglecting my home and family.

So in the good there is pain.

And I haven't been helped much by many Christian—or secular—books and articles aimed at women. I'm not the ideal contented housewife some Christian leaders portray. Neither am I the hard-charging senior manager straight out of the pages of business books. Yet I *am* ambitious and serious about work; I thrive on professional stimulation. But at the same time, I love being a wife and mother and consider myself a pro-family Christian who affirms traditional values. Who speaks for me? For us?

You see, I'm finding out I'm not alone. Not by a long shot.

Our tribe is increasing, and together we need help in dealing with these seeming contradictions. But to paraphrase poet Robert Frost, "Something there is that does not love a paradox." We are more comfortable with one thing *or* the other—good *or* bad, joy *or* pain.

Someone once said the mark of a first-rate mind is its ability to hold two opposing ideas simultaneously: *This is true, and this is also true.* I'm not yet there, but I do know life isn't always as simple or as pretty as the cozy portraits painted above. To paraphrase psychiatrist M. Scott Peck, "Life is complicated."

And getting more so. But I believe my family *and* my work are gifts from God. He did not include a user's manual, of course. That he left up to me. But he did leave me the broad guidelines of his Word; I am called to be faithful, to rely on his promises, to make him Lord of every area of my life.

And perhaps the tensions and complexities I grapple with, the choice between two goods, is an incalculable blessing that points me toward him.

Come with me now as I unfold a bit of my story—and perhaps yours too—as a woman who bumps through her too-short days, always juggling everything, always trying to keep a sense of humor about it all—who occasionally is touched by grace.

Wheaton, Illinois
March 1991

1

Hold On to
the Morning

*A*nd in the weather today: Clearing and colder . . ."
I shut the clock radio off. Five A.M. My husband
sleeps next to me, so quietly. I blunder through the
dark to put in my contacts, then get the coffee going—
first things first. I have an all-day conference to
attend, and I'm starting early.

While the coffee is brewing, I go outside to fetch the
paper and am nearly knocked over by a strong north
wind. There's something thrilling in its clean power, its
scent of glaciers and evergreens and hidden Canadian
lakes. I stand for a moment, sheltered by our front porch,
and look at a huge moon sinking in the west.

A ski-masked jogger thwaps by on the icy street.
Some people are really obsessed, I think, and go back into
my warm house for coffee and the newspaper.

I'm feeling unusually fresh today. Must have
slept well last night. Good thing; I'll need it at this
conference. I leaf through the paper but can't concentrate, so I look over the conference schedule and
study some notes I made.

Here I am at five-fifteen, working again. But it feels
right, this brisk morning. I think about my day and prickle
in anticipation: *There's a world out there, and I want it.*

Someone once asked me if I loved my job. I had
to give the question some thought. Finally I responded, "No. I enjoy my job—most of the time. But I
don't love the routine, the obligation to be someplace.
What I love is my work."

I make a list of the people I want to be sure to talk to
at the conference. I love the people my work brings into
my life; I love the variety of things I do. Most of all, I
love the creative stretching and flexing—as hard as it
is sometimes. And yes, it *is* nice to get paid for all this.

I look out the front window. The sky is beginning
to brighten, dimming the sinking moon. Don't be
fooled by the sun—it's *cold* out there. For a brief
moment I consider how nice it would be to stay home
and bake cookies instead of going off to work.

But there it is. I cannot be in two places at once, and I
am grateful to God for the many blessings he has sent my
way. Speaking of which, here comes my husband in
the blue terry robe I gave him for his birthday. We kiss,
talk about the weather. We don't say a lot, not this
early. But we don't need to. This is a beloved ritual,
this sharing of the morning—at least until the time
pressure's on and we become speeding human blurs.

After a while I go fix oatmeal, my special recipe
with brown sugar and cinnamon and a pat of un-
salted butter. The cereal's fragrance is nostalgic and
reassuring. Cold wind outside, hot oatmeal inside: I
like the rightness of it. I set the table and serve Fritz.
"Looks good!" he says (I told you we don't say a lot in
the morning).

"Boo!"

Here's Amanda now, carrying her sock-doll
monkey, Pippo. She joins us and eats enthusiastically,
offering some to Pippo, who declines.

Well, this *is* a moment!

Of course, it isn't always like this at our house, so I savor the peace. More often I'm hauling my daughter out of bed at the last minute while my husband grabs some yogurt on the fly. More often I am rushing out the door with my hair still wet from the shower.

I watch my husband, scraping the last bits of oatmeal from the bowl. I look at my daughter, drinking Juicy Juice. I look around at my kitchen, blue and white. I think of the conference and the new dress I bought at a post-Christmas sale.

Two gifts.

I have a family I adore—and work that can bring me joy. Maybe tomorrow I will have to rush to get ready; maybe I will be exhausted and resent the demands placed on me; maybe the sparkling snow will give way to slush and Amanda will come down with another ear infection.

But this morning of the new year is something to hold in the palm of my hand, something to carry me through the inevitable juggling act when I struggle with the discouragement fatigue brings.

As I get ready to leave, I notice a chickadee flitting about the evergreens outside my bedroom window. *Amazing how such little birds survive the winter*, I think. He whistles, "dee-dee-dee." And in the friendly chirping I seem to hear a tiny but unmistakable command: *Hold on to this morning!*

And I will.

The dress looks good. It's time to go. Hugs to my two loves, Fritz and Amanda. From one world to another . . . in the light of the morning.

2

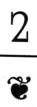

A Call? Is It for Me?

So why work?

Do most women work to put bread on the table—or to buy a third car? Is it true, as I have read, that the majority of women would work even if they didn't have to for financial reasons? What about a sense of calling?

Meet Beth.

Beth is tall, dark-haired, a talented musician. She teaches Sunday school and chairs her church's Christian education board. She has two school-age children, reads Dobson, and worries about society's moral decline.

Beth also works outside the home thirty hours a week for a Christian ministry. Money is very tight for her family; Beth's salary covers the rent on their home (they cannot afford to buy a house) and provides new hightops for her daughter. Beth's husband, Ron, is a salesman whose income is irregular—one year good, another bad. Last year was bad.

A few months ago I was in a group with Beth, talking about some of the struggles Christian families face today. Beth led off the discussion: "My greatest problem is that I'm a working mom, and I have to deal with people's attitudes toward that. I sense criticism. So I always tell them, 'I *have* to work. My husband's income just doesn't cover our needs.'"

As she spoke so candidly, I felt my face redden in anger at the judgments some cast at the working woman. I had to speak up: "You know, Beth, why is it we always feel compelled to add the I-have-to-work apology? Why can't we Christian women be honest about enjoying our work? Talk about what we do?"

"You're right," Beth said with surprise. "I enjoy my work, and I think I'm good at it. But somehow, that isn't enough for some people."

I doubt Beth would say she feels "called" to her work for an audio production studio. But she likes her work, she strives to be a conscientious employee, and her salary enables her family to live in modest comfort. Beth is not driven by me-first ambition—if anything, like most of us, she could use more self-esteem. She does not need darts of judgment shot her way.

My friend Charlotte has also wrestled with the have-to-work/like-to-work problem. Charlotte works as a meter reader for the electric company. Until recently she was a single parent supporting a son; now remarried, she continues to work for economic reasons. She gets up every day, puts on a uniform, and goes outdoors in all kinds of weather to dodge dogs and check meters. This is the type of work many women do, a job that by all appearances has little to do with one's Christian commitment. It's just a paycheck.

Charlotte, though, is also a singer and composer, a gifted musician who sings of matters close to her heart— her father's illness, the loneliness of the elderly, what God has done in her life. Charlotte would like to do more with her gift, but is hesitant about turning a private treasure into a public commodity. She needs the dependable salary her daily work provides—the economic rewards of being a Christian artist are anything but dependable.

   So for Charlotte, the call and the paycheck are
two separate entities. Yet she has managed to find
dignity in her work, something to be thankful for, and
she wrote a song about it:

Workboots

There they sit — across the floor
I put my workboots on — once more
And sometimes as I tie the knot
I'll think of those who haven't got
a job.

Oh, I've been given so much
I just don't know it
If thanks is deep inside —
Help me show it.

When winter comes — it comes too fast
I feel old.
I'll zip my coat — put on the hat
Out in the cold again.

But many are the people who know
nothing more
And hope for spring is never
waiting at their door.

And I complain too much — it seems
When I feel the storms destroy
my dreams.

Get bundled up in all my care
And never see the people
Shivering there.

Oh, I've been given so much
I just don't know it
If thanks is deep inside
Help me show it.

Charlotte, like Beth, has not had an easy time of it. She feels the pull of her art on the one hand, and her need for a regular paycheck on the other. But she is learning gratitude for the gift of good work, something that provides meaning—whether it is tinkering on a piano or tromping through backyards.

This notion of "calling" is complicated; it is often a word that gets bandied about too loosely. We sometimes say, "I feel the Lord has called me to this," when what we really mean is, *It's what I want.* Most of us do not have Scottish preacher Peter Marshall's experience of hearing God's call into the ministry on the night he was about to fall into a quarry. God's will for our lives is usually not that clear. We tend to stumble into a few quarries before we settle on the right path—or paths—for our lives. But still, there are clues and confirmations . . .

When I was four, I taught myself to read. I would show my mother words in magazines and newspapers and ask, "What does this say? What does this say?" It was as if I couldn't wait to get to school to unlock the puzzle of those black squiggles. I became an avid reader, one of those kids who always has her "nose in a book." English, spelling, and composition were almost embarrassingly easy for me, and I was happy doing them. I wrote occasional stories, but didn't know yet that people could put words on paper and get paid for it.

Then I turned into a teenager who disliked just about every aspect of life except books. Finally, in college, I began to write for the student newspaper. I found that I enjoyed it, that I did not have to work very hard at it, and that people I respected said good things about my efforts.

Years later, I had a conversation that had a powerful effect on my life. I was working on my first book and it was not going well. "How does one write a book?" I asked an author friend, a successful novelist, poet, and theologian with a hefty body of published work. "Am I doing what God would have me to do?"

My friend sat back, fixing me with blue eyes. I knew he understood; like me, he had been a gawky, sometimes miserable teenager in glasses. He knew, I think, how it was to speak not but see much.

I waited. He paused, then said, or rather pro-nounced, *ex cathedra*: "You should be writing books. You must write books."

He thinks I should write books!

Something inside me lifted, shifted. It was one of those high, epiphanic moments not often given to us. The chime in the mind: *You are this.* Usually we stumble along in a haze, guessing at our next move, grabbing at handholds and hoping for the best. Yet every once in a while the haze lifts and light slants down, and we climb toward it.

Thank you, I thought. *You have taken the time to give me a signal gift.*

I began to understand this gift, and the holiness of effort rightly committed, one night as I wrote at the kitchen table, on an almost superhuman deadline to finish a book chapter. To meet it, I had to pull an all-nighter. It was summer, and the windows were open. The house was quiet. I had the radio on low and was drinking coffee — with caffeine. I got up to walk around and listen to the night. Somewhere a screech owl called. A gnat flew around the light.

Then I sat down to write again, and it was as if all rational, daytime defenses were peeled away. I was tired, but I was also operating on an intuitive charge. The owl, the gnat, the night, and I — all about our wee-hours business. I wrote and wrote and wrote without stopping. The words just poured. I was finished by five, and my husband got up and we sat on our screened porch, read the paper, and watched a thunderstorm roll in.

Intuition, my foot. That was of God.

Of course, usually I, like Charlotte, put my "workboots" on and grumble about having to go to the office, where I push papers around and sit in meetings and develop neck cricks from talking on the phone so much. It doesn't feel very sacred; it feels rather humdrum. Have a good evening. See you tomorrow.

Yet there can be a beauty, a reassurance in the order and predictability of work. For some women I know (men too), work is a haven. These are people coping with horrendous burdens at home—an alcoholic husband, a mentally ill wife, a sullen teen. For such, the cheerful chatter of workmates may sound like the laughter of angels.

So we perform our tasks with a measure of gratitude. We may offer up a silent prayer at the beginning of our workday: *To you, the glory.* We look for ways to serve God, to help others. And yes—we enjoy what we do. Unapologetically.

3

Always a Full-Time Mom

*T*oday I am not feeling well, so I stay home from work. After sleeping away most of the morning, I help Amanda with her kindergarten "homework" — to find and cut out five pictures of things beginning with the letter *L*. We sit in our "story chair," the big wing chair in which I read to her at night, and look at ladies and legs and ladders and lakes and lettuce. Outside, a few flakes of snow start to drift down, presaging a deeper storm — something always welcome in our snow-loving household. A pair of cardinals and a few juncos and chickadees snack on seed in the front yard. I show Amanda which redbird is the mommy and which is the daddy.

The homework successfully completed, we play with refrigerator magnets. I demonstrate how you can make a metal object magically move on a wood table with the aid of a hidden magnet. I explain how electromagnetism makes the Northern Lights and has something to do with the earth's rotation. (Doesn't it? Well, it sounds good to her.)

Unhurried, relaxed hours. The house is reasonably tidy; the television is OFF. No "DuckTales" or "Rescue Rangers" or that guy selling carpets with that inane jingle.

Such a luxury, such a precious luxury, to be able
to look out the window with your child and say,
"Look! Suzie Snowflake!" To not speak to her in the
usual hurried, harried tones: Time to get up. Time to
go. Time for your bath. Get to bed. To see her content,
clearly glowing in the light of Mommy's attention.

It is then that I wonder, *Is this how it's supposed to be?
Am I happy because I'm doing what I should be doing?*

I'm not alone in this. All women worry about
their mothering, about how their kids are "turning out."
For those of us who work, when things do go wrong,
we're tempted to blame our careers: *If I didn't work, my
son wouldn't be getting D's in math. If I didn't work, she
would get to bed earlier. If I didn't work, I wouldn't have to
get my kids up at dawn, bundle them into snowsuits, and
haul them off to day care.*

Some of this is easily dismissed—I failed algebra
more times than I care to count, and my mother was a
full-time housewife (she didn't understand math,
either). Kids will punch each other out on the bus and
lose their homework and get acne and refuse to go to
bed. It happens, regardless of their parents' occupa-
tions. And there's no consensus on the importance of
a parent's constant presence around a child once that
child is past toddlerhood.

But the knife twists when we consider that, yes,
our preschoolers probably would be better off if they
weren't in day care. Our adolescents probably
shouldn't have to be alone every afternoon, locked in
the house and staring at MTV.

Leave the experts aside for a moment. What if we
have no other choice? What if we have to work full
time and cannot afford a home babysitting arrangement? What if there is no grandmother nearby to take
up the slack, no supportive spouse willing to juggle his

schedule for the sake of the kids? No spouse at all? Then we live with our choices and look for those moments of peace and contentment. We try to do our best, and we trust God for the rest.

Moments. A wise man and I once talked about how, amid this world's sorrow and suffering, moments like these must be accepted as a gift. "I think of our foster child," he said, "and I brood about the horrors of the system and about our fallen world. Then I look at my college-age daughter playing in the snow with him, and I know joy. You have to be ready for it."

Maybe I only need to receive a day like this with my child—to take it almost sacramentally—rather than flagellate myself with guilt (why don't I stay home so I can have this all the time?) and envy (housewives have all the fun!).

The moment passes, as moments do. Outside, the snow thickens and swirls. I go into the bedroom to work; Amanda runs off to play . . . happy, not battering at the door as she has been known to do. I think again of the statement I've heard so often from so many Christians—that when we stand before the Throne, God won't commend us on a work promotion, a sale made, a report (or book) completed. He will, however, call us to account for the special people he has placed in our lives.

Lord, when did we see you standing ready to throw a ball?

Last weekend I read an article by a columnist who described how she had been handed some massive editorial project with an impossible deadline. She was to finish it over the weekend—the weekend of her daughter's eighth birthday. She briefly considered

going for it, doing it all, skipping sleep and pleasing
both her boss and her child. She entertained the idea
of calling off the party. In the end, though, she told
her boss, "I can't do this." Her boss, annoyed, took on
the project herself.

Superwoman flunks again.

For many working women, these sacred moments have to come at the expense of something else.
You give a party, the article doesn't get written. You
chase butterflies with your kids, the kitchen floor stays
unscrubbed. It's almost punitive: you wanna dance, you
gotta pay the piper. With interest.

Then I remember Debbie White.

Debbie White is a very tall, striking black woman
with an all-embracing smile. Her daughter is in
Amanda's class. Debbie works in a factory — on the
day shift now, but in the fall she worked the night
shift. Yet she dropped Delma off in the morning and
picked her up at noon. She was always there helping
at class parties or chaperoning field trips. She and her
husband Tyrone even decorated the classroom on
Delma's birthday.

My husband and I once asked Debbie when she
slept. "Not often," she said. "But I figure it's just for a
few months. You can get through anything if you
know it's going to end."

Debbie does have family support; now Delma's
grandfather, a big, perpetually cheerful man, brings
her to school. But Debbie *is* doing it — being there for
Delma, keeping up with a job she needs. You do what
you have to do.

These are perilous times for our children; we
would be blind if we dismissed the dangers. However, I am convinced the majority of parents are
conscientious, committed, attentive — like Debbie
White. And let's look at our children for a moment. I

want to tell you about something that happened to my daughter.

She was in Sunday school, four years old. She was watching two other little girls play house when another child came up to them and asked, "Can I play with you?" "No, you can't," they replied nastily. The rejected child's eyes filled with tears; her lower lip trembled. Amanda went over to her, put her arm around her, and said, "I'll play with you, Annalyn." "You will?" Annalyn replied tremulously.

This is a good kid. These are all good kids.

You see, God is working in our children, and we can "parent" them only so much. Our children are not clay we breathe life into—that's already been done. I like the Steve and Annie Chapman song about how children (and grownups too!) "haven't turned out yet." They're growing, becoming—sometimes because of us, sometimes in spite. Yes, there are things we can do to help that along; for example, Amanda and I have "talking time" in bed, in the dark, before she goes to sleep. This time is inviolate; this is the time when confidences are shared, theology discussed, silly jokes told. It is never hurried or cut short. As much as we can, we need to give our kids our time, our selves.

But in the end, we're separate. "Train up a child in the way he would go"—not in the way we would have him go. That verse always reminds me of a morning-glory vine that needs to be trained upward or it will twine along the ground. But twine it will, and you can't force it into some unnatural position. You can help the morning-glory be the best it can be—but God does the rest.

The world is a different place than it was in the fifties, when I ran barefoot through open meadows of buttercup and clover and my greatest peril was getting spiked by a thistle or stepping on a nail. But we must trust—in our own good instincts, in our children themselves, and, finally, in God. They're his, after all.

And . . . there are always those moments. Look! The snow!

4

Can't We Just Be Friends?

*B*arbara is redheaded and slim. Her khaki slacks always have a perfect crease. She drives a new mini-van, the transportation of choice for families in my neck of the woods. Barbara looks like an all-American sorority girl, the perfect evangelical wife—but in reality she is far more intense and complicated. Not long ago she told me, "I don't feel as though I have many friends."

"But what about Sue?" I asked, naming a mutual acquaintance.

"She and I have nothing in common," Barbara said flatly.

Nothing in common. At first the statement surprised me; then, as I thought about it, I heard some of what was really being said. While Barbara and Sue are around the same age, both married to successful business executives, both parents of three children, both Christians, there's a deeper difference. Barbara is launching a photography career. She takes portraits, teaches at the community college, and exhibits her work in local galleries. She sees herself as wife, mother, *and* artist, and she struggles with the challenges of reconciling her various roles. Sue, on the other hand, while capable and talented in many areas, does not have a career outside the home and doesn't particularly want one.

For Barbara, that one difference meant everything. For her, it meant friendship wasn't possible.

Around the same time, I had a similar conversation with another woman, an at-home mother. Linda had driven me home from a church meeting, and we sat in her station wagon and talked in front of my house. Our conversation had that defenses-down candor peculiar to chats in cars in the dark hours. We spoke of relationships, loneliness, self-esteem. And she told me *she* felt she had very few close friends in our church.

This time I was really amazed. I had always thought that Linda cozily occupied the innermost ring of the inner circle, while I wistfully orbited the chilly outer reaches. Linda is Mercury; I am Neptune.

She told me she felt as if she could confide in me. "You make people feel . . . smart," she said. *You make me feel . . . wanted*, I thought, and was happy for the simple fact of reaching beyond the fact I have a profession outside the home and Linda does not.

Lately I've been realizing I have few friends who are stay-at-home moms like Linda. The women I do no-agenda lunches with, the women I enjoy gabby phone conversations with, the women I make room for in my crowded life, tend to be professionals who work part time, full time, or freelance. The few college friends I have kept up with over the years all work. Even my mother works.

There is black-haired Maureen, working on her first book. We talk about the writing life, but we also worry about our bodies and share an affinity for zinger wisecracks. I call her when I'm having a nobody-loves-me attack, and she cheers me up by telling me her troubles. Then we start laughing about something.

Others. Ruth Anne, at home now with a new baby after working for years. Two-decade friend Virginia, earning her doctorate and trying to survive teenagers — one of them handicapped. And hazel-eyed Sandy, so lovely, so unsure of herself.

I have heard of "Mommy Wars." I have heard (though never experienced firsthand) that career women are stung by housewife smugness, that housewives feel looked down upon by their working counterparts. I don't know. Some of the split between the two groups is based upon simple logistics: someone like Sue or Linda sees friends at a morning Bible study; someone like me does lunch. But the instinct to cluster, like with like, enters in here, too. We all are more at ease when we share certain assumptions, a silent common language. And for those of us who are professionals, the fact is, we like talking about our work — and we like to talk about it with others who appreciate what we do all day.

Such thinking, however, ignores the fact that God created us as more than walking job descriptions. We are more than our career yearnings or professional achievements. And we are more than our role as mother or wife.

I am not entirely comfortable in the world of at-home mothers, especially moms in large groups with little kids. I occasionally take my daughter to McDonald's, but I don't enjoy it much. We sit on the playground when weather permits. I eat alone, picking at my chicken salad, while Amanda jumps into the orange balls. I am conspicuous in my skirt and earrings, while all around me mothers, sometimes in pairs, are dressed in jeans or sweats or shorts. They feed their kids, yell at their kids, herd their kids. I feel like the sore — albeit salaried — thumb.

When I covertly observe the other moms, this thought arises unbidden: *I'm glad I don't have to do this*

all day. Oh, I love playing with my child. I love having
her playmates over and creating tea parties for them
and in general acting like the Nicest Mom in the
Neighborhood. I would like to do it more.

But I have not made a career out of being a
mother. More important, I don't *see* myself as a mother
above all with my work being incidental. Even sitting
in McDonald's, I can feel my two heads.

So no, we are not our jobs. But the thing we
spend most of our day doing, the way we see ourself,
is bound to rub off on our personalities and show up
in our conversations. It will affect our perceptions of
other people, and theirs of us.

A journalist researching an article on peer pressure once asked me if I sensed tacit — or overt —
hostility from at-home women because of my career.
Unlike Beth, my friend who admitted being hurt by
such criticism, I had to tell the interviewer, "No, I
really haven't sensed such hostility, unless I'm blind
or naive." But what I *have* sensed is a bemused, even
distanced (and distancing) admiration: "Oh, you
work, you write, you have a family — how do you do
it all? You must be very busy." Yes, I am. End of
conversation. And when this happens, I almost feel as
if I've experienced a sort of cross-cultural encounter:
Tell me about your native customs.

That's one reason I'm fond of Linda. Around her
I don't feel like an alien. Linda radiates a warm acceptance of those around her, a sort of shrugging
disregard for status, role, position. She just doesn't
concern herself with such externals.

Still, even Linda has trouble connecting. Could it
be the "Mommy Wars" so extensively covered and
exploited by the media mask something deeper, a
thirsting loneliness? Women are supposed to be the
masters of the relational, surrounded by warm closeness.

But after listening first to Barbara and then to Linda—as well as several other women over the past months—I'm not so certain.

In many ways Linda's life is not mine. She married younger, has more kids, a larger house, more organized closets. She plays the piano with fire and brilliance, and I never got beyond "Heart and Soul." We are, I suspect, driven by different engines—I more restless, Linda more content with who she is.

But the things that unite us are greater than those that separate us. So too with photographer Barbara and the scorned Sue. "Nothing in common?" The things we can give each other are more important than our varying "lifestyles." Linda and I can help each other, listen to each other, learn from each other. Sue can do the same for Barbara, and Barbara for Sue. And, as busy as we all are, we can be friends. And that, too, is a gift.

5

Loving the Good,
Living with the Bad

*L*ife sure gets complicated. Finding time for friends,
making time for family, wondering if I should
change jobs . . . are these things gifts from God, or
insoluble nuisances? How can we love the "good" we've
been given while accepting the "bad" that comes with it?

The other day I came across a quote from Thomas Merton, the author/monk who renounced the
life of a cosmopolitan intellectual for the rigors of a
Trappist monastery. He wrote of himself, "I have
become convinced that the very contradictions in my
life are in some ways signs of God's mercy to me."

Merton, of course, was not a two-headed woman.
He did not have to juggle the passions for work and
home, job and family. He was, however, continually
pulled between his desire for a life of tranquil reflection, on the one hand, and active engagement with
the world, on the other. Merton was torn between the
cloister and the street.

Thomas Merton was instrumental in my becoming a Christian. I loved his intellectual richness, his
faith tempered by worldly experience. If he could
believe, I could believe. No simple formulas for
Merton. I liked that—and I like it now.

And as a Christian, I turn to God's Word for
answers—and find complexity spilling over page
after page after page. I find paradox: this . . . *and*
that. I see it in David, mighty king *and* fallen sinner.
In Peter, who denied his Lord *and* died for him. And I
find it in the list of basic biblical truths all Christians
affirm. New Testament scholar Klyne Snodgrass
points these out:

- The Kingdom of God is in our midst. It
  has not yet arrived.
- Christ won the victory at Calvary. Yet we
  are a fallen race, and the victory will not
  be complete until he comes again in glory.
- By grace you are saved through faith.
  Faith without works is dead.

A few Sundays ago, we were discussing the Book
of Romans at church. We got into a lively debate
about what it feels like to be a Christian and why, if
we have new life in Christ, we still sin—and enjoy it.
"Why doesn't being a Christian always feel the way
it's supposed to?" challenged one man. The class
leader responded with a phrase that shouts paradox:
"You have to think of it in this way: `Now and not
yet.'"

Now and not yet. Two equal truths.

How does this help all the women like me who
struggle with resolving the pull in different directions?

First, it is comforting to remember that the complexities and tensions of life find their echo in
Scripture. Yet it is a complexity undergirded by
abiding belief and affirmation. Scripture doesn't leave
the ambiguity unresolved; it says, in effect, that there
are no easy little answers—only one big Answer.

God created complexity. Consider the workings of the human brain, the intricacies of the chambered nautilus, the various forces that keep the earth from spinning off in space. He offers creative tension and multiple answers as a gift, I believe—to encourage us to ask more questions, to live with richness, to come closer to him as we try to piece the puzzle together. And, since we won't piece the puzzle together on this side of forever, complexity and unanswered questions keep us humble before the Lord, aware of our neediness and lack of knowledge.

And because God made us, we, too, are complex, hard to categorize. No one is all one thing. I think we sometimes forget that, influenced as we are by the media's tendency to oversimplify: Mommy Wars. Conservative traditionalist. Superwoman. Radical feminist.

I know *I'm* not all one thing. For example, last night I clipped recipes and coupons, whipped up pancake batter for breakfast, rearranged knickknacks, and read a newspaper account of those fighting to protect the rights of the unborn. I thought about work and peeked at my sleeping daughter. That's a typical weekday evening for me.

And the more women I talk to, the more complexity I discover. "This isn't me," I hear. "And this isn't me. So what about the rest of us?"

You're human.

The discovery of complexity, of the pain that comes with many good gifts, can free us from corrosive guilt, worry, frustration, from thinking we should manage our lives better. It's *okay* to feel pulled in different directions, to sometimes wonder *Who am I, really? Where do I fit in?* It's okay to sense that God has called us to two arenas, two responsibilities that sometimes conflict with each other. It's okay not to have all the answers, or even very many answers. Or to have two answers that bump into each other. And in a way, it keeps life more interesting—and possibly more as God intended it.

6

Have a Nice Evening

I am so tired I feel as if pebbles are grinding into my corneas. From the back. So I'm in no mood to wait for my husband, who's late to pick me up from work. I thought I would stand outside the office and wait in some fresh air.

But boy, is this air fresh. Must be all of ten degrees. And me without my hat. It's actually a nice-looking royal-blue knit that matches my coat, but often I refuse to wear it because it flattens my hair like an old Beatles wig.

Except today I got my hair cut stylishly short and my ears are totally exposed. I have heard that cold metal earrings contract, making them pinch. Pinch? They feel like industrial clamps. I take them off and go stand in the lee of the building.

I feel like a fool. Who hangs around outside the office after hours when the wind chill is in double negative numbers? I skip a little and think of the Jack London story we read in high school, the one where the guy lights his last match to build a warming fire . . . and is later found frozen to death, just yards from his cabin.

Here Fritz comes. I can hear the car now; it's making some sort of screech, probably something in the steering system. *Oh, please God, don't let it be any-thing major. This is a tight month for us.*

Be nice, Betsey, I tell myself. I was a shrew this morning, late and screaming and flinging clothes all over the bedroom. Chalk it up to raging hormones. What a great excuse we women have!

He pulls up with a sheepish smile. I jump in, barely greeting my daughter, who waits with a bright, hopeful face. "What's wrong with the car?" I shrill.

He thinks it's a belt or something. Take it in tomor-row. Meanwhile, here we are, making this humiliating racket, like we're derelicts driving a beater. Like a teenager, I imagine everyone is staring and pointing.

Our parakeets are out of seed, so we stop at two convenience stores. They don't have it. I wail that the birds will starve and hate myself for not being more organized. My daughter looks at me, baffled. *Who is this woman?*

Home, finally. The birds perch forlornly by their seed cups. Sorry, guys. I step on cracker crumbs and they crunch into the carpeting. My mother-in-law is coming over tomorrow and we haven't vacuumed. Or dusted. Or scrubbed the bathroom. Newspapers litter the living room. I rush to straighten up and my daughter whines for a cookie. "Just a minute!" I snap. Pick up, put away. Night after night after night.

I decide to change into jeans. They say you can ease the after-work transition by changing out of your work clothes right away. I toss my dress into the hamper and forcibly shove the laundry down. The hamper is so full the wicker is unraveling. I think of some well-known Christian women I admire and wonder if they ever step on cracker crumbs or have undone laundry. Probably not.

My daughter reminds me she has homework to do. We have to tape one hundred paper clips to poster board to demonstrate counting by tens. I sigh. *This is gonna be a long night.*

Dinner is microwaved leftovers. Amanda turns up her nose at them and contents herself with juice and yet another cookie. The phone rings during dinner, and my husband answers it. "Hello? Oh, yes, sorry about that. We'll get it in the mail tomorrow."

Now to the paper clips, which take forever. My husband does the dishes. I have hardly said two civil words to him. I imagine the parakeets are staring balefully at me; I can feel their tiny black eyes boring into my back. Living reminders of my inadequacy. Let's see. We're at seventy now. Amanda wants to draw a heart around each paper clip. I dissuade her. Eighty, ninety . . .

She wants a story, and it's now after eight. I mechanically read to her from *Winnie-the-Pooh*. Fritz gets her into her nightgown while I sit for a minute, the first minute I've had to myself all day. The pebbles behind my corneas are starting to feel like boulders. I gaze around at the clutter. The house looks dusty and neglected—like the birds that are pecking on the bottom of their cage. I think of documentaries I've seen about animals in Africa desperately foraging across a drought-stricken landscape.

It is now nine and I'm just getting my child to bed. Amanda coughs. I hope she's not getting sick; I can't stay home tomorrow. I cuddle next to her, feeling guilty for the thousandth time, wondering if she gets enough sleep, wondering if all this is worth it. There must be a better way. Well, at least she has her paper clips to take tomorrow.

Once Amanda is down for the night, I think about turning on the television or leafing through the newspaper or talking to my husband. I do none of these. I attack the clutter. I briefly consider laying out my clothes for the next day, as the working-woman advice articles say you should, but the state of my closet depresses me. And I don't iron unless I'm desperate.

I sit again and think of an illustration I saw in a magazine. An exhausted woman sprawls in a chair, holding a copy of the *New York Times*. The front-page headline announces, "MOM TAKES A NAP!"

I still haven't talked much to my husband. It will have to wait; he's tired too and I need to be up before dawn tomorrow to work on a book project. We both fall into bed. I know I will be asleep in minutes and remember reading somewhere that if you nod off as soon as your head hits the pillow, you're running a sleep deficit. Hmmm. Fritz and I exchange a good-night kiss and lights out. Tomorrow is another day . . .

7

"I'll Always Be Around"

I 've just seen what love looks like. Maybe even what God looks like.

I was curled up on Amanda's bed. The night light was on—the light author J. M. Barrie called "a mother's eyes." We were talking quietly, confidentially; I was telling her that years ago there were some people in a former church who didn't much like her daddy or me. She reached out and almost smothered me in a hug. "Those bad people!" she said indignantly. "I'd hit them!

"I love everything about you," she continued. "I love your hair, your eyes, your mouth, your shoulders, your neck, your arms . . ."

Quite simply, she loved me. And she told me so. "I'll always be around," she said. "Except when I'm at school!"

Suddenly I was tearing up, weeping at this quite startling, unsolicited, wonderful rush of acceptance. I realized again how encumbered I sometimes feel, how I don't get hugged very much, how I can ache from the weariness of being pulled in so many directions. *Where does this come from? How did she know?*

I finally said good night to her. And she hugged me again, this time quietly and firmly. I allowed myself to be cared for by my child. I allowed myself to be fragile.

Little children, let us love one another.

Is this what God thinks of me? Do I sometimes need
to be still and know that I am loved, that I am worthy,
that I have a place to rest and weep and not be ashamed?

I'm not very good at this sometimes. It pleases
me to think of myself as the giver, the nurturer, the
initiator of love. (Can I dish it out and not take it?)
And when love does come, I sometimes prefer it
wrapped up in a compliment, a salary bonus, an
invitation to write an article. Tell me I look good, tell me I
perform well. That's the language I understand.

But love me for who I *am*? Unconditionally, expect-
ing nothing in return? There's something almost scary
about that, something I want to push away and hide from.

Why is this? Am I afraid of being found out? Do I
fear such pure love will shine a searchlight on my
soul and find it wanting? Or by standing still and
merely receiving, I relinquish my cherished control?

This is the truth: If I don't have anything to worry
about, I will invent something. I'm not sure I would know
how to deal with simple peace if it looked me in the eye.

Yet there peace was, nightgowned and tousle-
haired, holding me in the pink bedroom with the
Winnie-the-Pooh poster looking down. (Interesting:
Amanda's arms are now long enough to wrap all the
way around me.) The nurtured becomes the nurturer.

What wondrous love is this? . . .

Sometimes, perhaps, all we can do is stand in awe of
that love. And in a child's words, "I'll always be
around," I heard an echo: *For lo, I am with you always.*

I have read the promise often enough. Now I
have seen it. I do not quite understand it, but maybe I
am beginning to accept it — and receive it in humility.

8

In Search of a
Date Night

I t takes a half-dozen calls, but we finally secure a babysitter. We drop Amanda off and head for downtown Chicago. The sun is bright; there's a hint of spring in the air. We join the eastbound stream of traffic, our spirits high.

Alone at last.

And we are on our way to the hospital, where my father has spent the last month following brain surgery.

This is not my idea of "couple together time." This is not my idea of a date. A family crisis has forced my husband and me to back away from our normal routines, to deal with the frustration (and expense) of sitters, leave the housework and the writing and the painting projects behind, and *do* something together, just the two of us.

But hey, whatever it takes.

Once in the city, we crawl along Sheffield Avenue. Creep, stop. Creep, stop. Saturday morning on the North Side. I am just thinking about how much we have been driving lately, and how the more one is on the road the greater one is at risk for accidents, when *Wham!* the car behind us rams our back end.

Thanks to seat belts, we aren't hurt—just shaken up. A can of pop spills onto the upholstery. My husband jumps out to inspect the damage and talk to the offending driver, a young woman. I sit, staring straight ahead as passing motorists slow down to rubberneck. *I do not believe this.*

Incredibly, neither car is scratched. So we continue on, and decide to grab a bite of lunch before visiting Dad. There's a Cuban restaurant near the hospital I've been wanting to try. Shellfish and black bean soup sound mighty inviting about now.

But La Habana is closed, as is a pizza place nearby. We stroll around the neighborhood, dodging puddles. My shakiness goes away and I start feeling almost freewheeling. Just a couple of footloose kids, out for a good time in the city. We admire the colorfully renovated rowhouses and peer at the shops. The street life down here is great, in contrast to the dozing suburbs.

That's us, I think ruefully. *Dozing in the 'burbs.* We used to do this all the time before we were married — explore, risk, *go.* What happened? *What happens?*

We were adventurers, this man and I. He was in seminary in an urban neighborhood; I worked downtown. We didn't have a house. We didn't have a kid. We could spend on good times without worrying about our budget. Back then we frequented ethnic restaurants — Hungarian, Middle Eastern, Polish, Japanese, even British. We saw all kinds of movies, took long drives, walked on the beach in winter, when the wind whips up fantastic ice formations and makes your blood sing with aliveness. We heard blues and jazz and watched the Cubs and Sox lose and attended gatherings in black churches and were not afraid.

Now a bit of that adventurous feeling was starting to creep back in. We finally found an Indian restaurant open and went in, the only customers. We were ushered to a very private, very comfortable booth. As we sampled lamb rogan josh, tandoori chicken, yogurt and nan bread, and a wonderful dessert that tasted like dry ice cream, I could feel the burdens of my life drain away. It was wonderful not to be at work. It was wonderful not to be at home. My husband and I kept eating and smiling, eating and smiling. At each other.

When we left I felt energized, heartened, somehow aired out, as if the onrushing spring was blowing into the crevices of my soul. A good meal with your love will do that for you—especially when it's been a long time since you really enjoyed yourself.

One of the many tensions of living with multiple demands is that there are only so many hours in a day. When you work outside the home, a significant portion of those hours is spent at your office, on your factory shift, in your classroom, or on your hospital unit. Sleeping and eating and showering take time. Chores take time. Driving takes time.

What's left often goes to the children. Most women bend over backward to make time for their kids—helping them with their homework, reading them stories, feeding them, bathing them, chauffeuring them.

Guess who's forgotten?

A letter I read in "Dear Abby" made me stop and think. A woman described how her husband had died while she was on a business trip. He had been recovering from a mild heart attack; she had promised him that they would spend time together when the press of business allowed. Now it was too late, and she was alone with her regret.

It's tempting to point fingers at women who have no business traveling when they should be home with their spouse. But instead, the story raises a question for

me: What is life really for? Love, work, some ideal
combination thereof? Can love of spouse and need to
work be accommodated somehow? And how *do* we
find time together so that our date times aren't con-
fined to hospital visits?

Everyone says you should put love first, but few
actually do it. The machine must be fed, the engines
stoked. What if we downsized all our work commitments? This country would be about as economically
competitive as Bolivia.

And I know a mature marriage is woven of
shared responsibilities, mutual commitments, common tasks. Who needs romance after nearly thirteen
years? Can't a seasoned marriage function on cruise
control? And in truth I really do not need to be show-
ered with roses, taken out every week, barraged with
the proverbial love-note-in-the-briefcase. "Show your
love for me by making dinner," I have occasionally
said to my husband.

Yet how profoundly I need him. Not just as a
partner in the "enterprise" of our marriage, not just as
father to our child, not just as earner of income. *Him.*

One night not long ago I felt quite alone. The
grind of work, the sadness of my father's illness, my
depression over numerous undone house chores had
wholly depleted me. I felt like a lost little girl looking
for a home. I tried to pray, but God seemed remote,
preoccupied with other concerns. And, in the words
of the child terrified by the storm, I wanted comfort
"with skin."

Where would I find it? Who would console me
during my storm? And there he was, in mismatched
pajamas and evening stubble, lying on his side of the
bed, waiting to hold me and do for me what absolutely
no one else can do as well. Waiting, really, to be Christ
for me. I need more of these consolations. So does he.

Because, Lord willing, this man and I are going to be together for a long, long time. I would like to look back and think we made some of the right choices. I do not want to be like the businesswoman who wrote to "Dear Abby."

What *do* I want my marriage to look like after forty or fifty years—after careers have faded, the tumult has stilled, the children are gone? I remember our neighbors down the street. They live in a white house with big crabapple trees in the front yard. The trees turn a dazzling pinky-white in spring, and oh, the fragrance! But they don't get out much to enjoy their yard. He is an invalid and she cares for him.

A few weekends ago, my daughter and I went out for a walk. As we approached the white house, we saw the wife out painting porch furniture, her husband in a chair enjoying the sunshine. We chatted briefly. After a few minutes I had to run off to chase Amanda. But I was moved by the couple, by their mutual devotion. And it occurred to me, not for the first time: *What if this was us?* What if we were no longer busy, no longer in demand? What if the phone, always ringing, fell silent? What if the only head I sported was that of wife?

Such questions make me uneasy, because it is difficult to imagine *not* being busy. I don't ever want to have to retire from writing. But there may come a time when our lives are quieter, when it is just Fritz and I, sitting in the sunshine.

With the help of a gracious God, whose idea marriage was in the first place, I trust and pray that I *could* live with the quiet. But I can do more than that. I can start right now by making sure my marriage is not relegated to the margins of a crowded life.

I'm slowly learning that you do have to be rather intentional about this. I have tended to laugh at such

advice as "pencil your mate into your calendar." But
if you simply rely on spontaneity, you might be
waiting a long time. It was one thing when we were
courting—but it's tough to be spontaneous with a six
year old and several careers between you.

We've had our share of failed getaway weekends,
to be sure; anniversaries that have been a bust and
birthdays that have disappointed. But that's no reason
not to make the effort simply to *be with* each other. So
we try, and succeed more often than not, to spend
quiet time together early in the morning, right after
work, and—occasionally—before bedtime. We talk on
the phone. We chatter while we clean.

We're still working on date nights, and we need
to work harder in that area, because here's another
thing I'm learning: as I do my work/family juggling
act, I'm really not having enough fun. Most things I
do have a purpose, are geared toward accomplishing
something or helping someone. When I do have fun,
it's almost as an accidental by-product—laughter in a
meeting or being amused by my daughter's antics in
the bath. It makes me think I really ought to pencil
my spouse into my pocket calendar—if I had one.

Even when we're not having fun for fun's sake,
work does give us more to talk about, more to love
and respect in the other. Sometimes Fritz counsels
couples in our home. When I observe his patience, his
insightful questioning, and his ability to put people at
ease, I think, *Wow.* That's a great way to feel about
your spouse—and it doesn't happen often enough.

And I share my work with him. Together we
have entertained publishers and literary agents and
many other work friends in our home. I whine about
work, or, more often, tell him a joke I heard at the
office. He encourages me to write and reads what I
create. I could not do this alone.

We dream, too. We talk of writing a book together, a devotional series or a children's book. We discuss ways we can further mesh our worlds. Our marriage thrives on these dreams, on this crackling interchange between two good minds.

So we're not really dozing off in the suburbs. True, it's a different kind of adventure than the one we embarked on while we were courting—but it's deeper, more satisfying. We'd love more time together, but we're learning to make the most of the time we do have—which, God willing, will be for life.

Pass the curry, please.

9

Man of Sorrows

*T*he waiting room outside the intensive care unit at
the large city hospital is completely unadorned.
Two couches, gray. Two tables, no more than white
blocks. Carpeting with dots. Not even a plastic plant
to relieve the barrenness. I can't even find an old issue
of *People* magazine and read about E.T. or Oliver North.
When the elevator bell rings, everyone looks up; an
aide passing through with a laundry cart becomes
absorbing entertainment. Anything, perhaps, to take
the mind off what's going on past the double doors
that open by themselves. The air smells, not like
antiseptic solution or disease, but—disconcertingly—
like someone is sneaking a smoke in the rest room.

Which is probably why the man sitting next to me
wants to talk. He looks young-old: graying hair and
an aging body with an oddly fresh face that in a sad
way indicates a lifelong being-cared-for by someone else.
His mother, eighty-five, is dying, he says. She injured
her leg, then aspirated some substance and lapsed
into a coma. His blue boy-man eyes fill as he says, "I
don't know where I'll go, what will happen to me."

He is fifty-three, never married, has always lived
with his mother. "Once I had a chance," he confides.

"I was thirty-nine. But my father got sick, so the wedding was called off, and . . . well . . . "

He has not held a job in twenty years, he says. His mother will leave behind an "estate" of five hundred dollars and a house in a declining neighborhood. What will become of him—an only child, no other living relatives?

He looks at my daughter. "Your daughter is beautiful," he remarks. "She has pretty blonde hair. Does she look like you or your husband?"

Thank you. Probably a combination.

"Yes—yes, I can see that. So—you live in Wheaton? I was there once. There's a college there, right? College used to pretty much run things, I heard. Couldn't even have a movie theater in town."

Well, we have one now. A small one, of course.

I look at the elevator bank, hoping a maintenance person will emerge and amuse me with the jangling of his keys so I will not have to . . . what? Listen to this man? Console him?

Often, too often, I am tongue-tied in the presence of sorrowing need.

"What's wrong with your dad?" he asks.

Brain surgery. Doing better, they tell us. Not out of the woods yet, but . . .

"That's good."

Over the past fortnight I have been dwelling in my own valley of the shadow, unaware of all anguish save my own. *O Lord, this has been hard. Crushingly hard. This one I cannot glibly explain away.* God has been . . . somewhere.

Hard, hard, And yet.

Oh, I don't like the way he is looking at my daughter. (I wouldn't leave Amanda alone with this guy for five minutes!)

This man has no daughter.

Soon he will have no parents.

He has no spouse to cry against. No job to go to, no cheerful, humming routine to take his mind off the grieving. No brother or sister to trade old childhood jokes with.

When I leave this place, I will get on an expressway and follow the setting sun west into a county of office complexes, rolling fields, and restored downtowns. I will drive up a tree-lined street, turn the corner, flick open the automatic garage door, and walk into a house whose market value, we are told, has appreciated thirty thousand dollars in three years. Friends will phone, invite us over to parties, ask us to serve on church committees, inquire after Dad. I will sleep next to my husband in a queen-sized bed while my daughter breathes sweetly in her pink room, Raggedy Ann at her side. The loudest sound we will hear will be the scrape of the snowplow or the thrum of the furnace.

This boy-man, I notice, talks to all the newcomers in the sixth-floor waiting room—whether they hear him or not. It's probably less lonely here than where he has to go. I picture him getting on the elevated train and taking it to a dingy block in some neighborhood beset by panhandlers, crack addicts, prostitutes. He'll probably go up to his apartment or into his little house—after negotiating three deadbolt locks—and turn on "Wheel of Fortune." The phone will not ring—except, perhaps, when the word comes down from the hospital. Then arrangements will have to be made.

My husband comes out to relieve me. I look at him gratefully and flee into the sanctuary of my dad's hospital room. Away from sorrow; away from need.

Yes, here is sadness, but it is a sadness softened by hope and cushioned by much support. It is hard, but we will manage.

Others may not.

Ah, I am so petty sometimes, with my shallow thirtysomething concerns about working (. . . at least I have work) and mothering (. . . a child) and being a good wife (. . . a husband).

What would Jesus think? I'm not sure I want to know.

Later, my husband tells me, "You know what that man in the waiting room said? He said, `You have a nice wife.'"

10

Why I Said Yes to the Church Committee

When the phone rang at ten at night, I jumped. During my father's hospitalization, I had come to hate our phone's modest peeping. I picked up the receiver slowly and answered reluctantly.

"Betsey? This is Ted Ericson. I'm calling on church business. I was wondering if you would . . ."

I listened, leaning as I always do toward saying no. Asked my stock question: "What would this involve?"

Our denomination was launching a major fund-raising campaign. Every church was forming a local committee to boost the effort. I like Ted, and he was persuasive—so I said yes.

Of course, I probably had no business agreeing to serve. My tendency is to rashly say yes, then live to regret it. I'm always flattered to be wanted, and I dislike turning people down. But between work and family, my time is pretty much booked.

So whose isn't?

There are days when I feel like I'm shuttling mindlessly, like a mole, on a track between job-and-home, work-and-family, unaware of anything that falls outside my narrow world. Strife in the Baltic states?

I have no idea; ask me if I have any stockings without runs. The vanishing animals of the Serengeti? What is that compared to my vanishing checkbook balance?

I brood about this tunnel vision. I worry when I read that my Baby Boom generation is disinclined toward volunteerism. I get upset when I am told that book and magazine consumers want immediate, what's-in-it-for-me application out of what they read. Much has been written about the phenomenon of "cocooning." Sociologists tell us we're becoming a society of people who huddle in front of our VCRs, pay little attention to politics, and barely know our neighbors. It's a threatening world out there, so let's turn our backs on it and tend to our own walled gardens.

And so the village green, the public square, slowly disappears. We're afraid to talk to strangers. The old corner filling station where retired men used to sit and shoot the breeze has been replaced by a mini-mart. You can't get a flat tire fixed, but you can microwave a ham on rye. Most younger men don't join Lions or Kiwanis. There aren't enough at-home moms to lead Girl Scout troops. We don't sit on front porches and wave at passersby, because many of us don't have porches—and passersby have taken to their cars.

I'm sympathetic to much of this because I recognize my own desire to cocoon. I don't necessarily want to go out at night after a long day at work. Wouldn't it be selfish of me to leave my daughter just to attend a church meeting? They can always get someone else. So I retreat behind the walls of my house, eat dinner, read Amanda a story, talk to my husband, do chores. The world's needs will just have to do without me.

But what if everyone felt like this?

Times *have* changed since my mother raised children in the fifties. Economic pressures have forced women, the traditional backbone of the American volunteer force, into the workplace.

Nevertheless, while the Bible doesn't speak directly to the time pressures faced by today's women, Scripture does repeatedly call us to a life of service. Follow me. Leave your nets. There is a broader family crying out.

There is no getting around this scriptural mandate. The call rings from Deuteronomy, with its injunctions to care for the widows and orphans, to Matthew 25 and Jesus' concern for "the least of these."

And, what at first blush seems to be another burden to crowd into our lives may actually be a blessing.

Why? Because the jump off the shuttle, the involvement in an activity beyond ourselves, provides what I call a "third thing" — something that can help balance our work-and-family dilemma. It's another commitment, another love. But it's also a refreshing break from the routine — and it can make us less selfish.

I think of a man I know whom I'll call Paul. Paul commutes into the city to a demanding job in an accounting firm. He has a large family and could be excused if he shunned other commitments. But Paul finds time to direct his church's adult education program, serve on the board of a Christian school, counsel couples with financial problems, *and* play basketball or softball. Paul is one of those lanky, high-energy types who thrives on a packed Day-Timer. He's constitutionally made to be on the go.

But he also has a commitment to serve, an almost old-fashioned sense of duty. His workaday world deals largely with numbers, balance sheets, money for its own sake, so he needs a corrective to the greed he comes up against each day. Paul finds it in doing for

others—and I have a feeling he's spiritually and
emotionally healthier for it.

Most of us cannot be Paul. We who are mothers
of young children *are* needed by our families, and
building strong families is vital to a healthy society.
Yet most of us are not in danger of neglecting our
families for the sake of the wider world. And we
teach our children important lessons when they see us
helping out at a church workday, stirring batter at a
PTA pancake breakfast, tutoring a refugee in English,
or even just taking the time to listen carefully to a
lonely neighborhood child. (Amanda: "Why did you
talk to Danielle more than me?" Me: "Because, as
we've talked about, she has a sad situation at home
and she needs a nice mom to help her sometimes.")

We have to choose carefully. One friend I know
limits her extracurricular commitments to those that
benefit her sons—school, Scouts. Another friend,
who, like Paul, works in the financial world, has
served as treasurer for several organizations. We
cannot do it all . . . but we ought, perhaps, to do
something.

I recently read Karen Burton Mains' *Friends and
Strangers.* I was impressed by what Mains, who
knows firsthand the problem of having two heads,
said about her need to be involved with her small
Episcopal church: "The people of St. Mark's parish
have allowed me to become myself. . . . Karen
Mains, small group member, housewife, mother,
co-worker, wedding guest, committee co-chair,
potluck planner, name on the church supper sign-
up sheet, part of the cleaning crew, the last one on
the prayer chain, Sunday school teacher. I am part of
the life of this body. . . . My struggles and successes
are known to them; their pain and joys are known to
me."

I think back to an all-church workday I attended a couple of springs ago to mark Earth Day. It was the first really gorgeous Saturday in April. The marshy area behind our church was alive with birds. Our small-but-willing group of twenty gathered for a brief service, then scattered to our various tasks. I elected to weed so I could be outdoors. Others washed windows, scrubbed the kitchen, dusted sanctuary seating. One of the men took the children for a "nature walk." As I bent down and tried to pull out creeping Charlie, I drank in the smell of the awakening soil. Then Fritz and I picked up roadside litter as passing motorists looked on. Afterward, we stood around the kitchen eating hot dogs and discussing ways the church could do its part for the environment.

I could have stayed home and cleaned. I could even have taken Amanda to the playground. But I would not have felt nearly as good, as alive, as renewed.

I know other people who serve on park district boards, who take in foster children, who are active in Christian-advocacy causes such as protesting questionable textbooks. Interestingly, these are usually people who are *already* busy—and think nothing of adding another event to their schedule. But I see them as living full, enriching lives.

I know I can become way too preoccupied with *my* work, *my* house, *my* family, *my* life. Me. It isn't healthy, it isn't scriptural, and it drains me almost dry sometimes. Doing for others, with others, replenishes the well.

A few weeks after I heard from Ted, we gathered at his house for the first meeting. I walked over on a starry night, cheerfully leaving my family behind. We sat in his living room with the marble fireplace and collection of well-thumbed books; a friendly cocker spaniel nuzzled our hands for attention. We talked about the campaign, set goals, made plans. But *what* we discussed was, for me, less important than the satisfying feeling of stretching myself. Right off the shuttle.

11

I Want to Be Alone (Sometimes)

G o to sleep. Mommy loves you." I leave the door partly ajar and tiptoe out. It is nearly nine o'clock, late for a kindergartener to be getting to bed. *Please God, let her go to sleep.* She needs it—and I need her to be asleep. So I can be alone and enjoy it while I'm still conscious.

My husband is already in his robe and pajamas. "I'm tired, love. I'm going to hit the sack."

"Oh . . . okay." I decide to call my mother and settle down at the kitchen table for a good chat. We are engaged in an animated discussion when a sprite in a Little Mermaid nightshirt bursts into the room. *Oh, no.*

Raggedy Ann has fallen to the floor. She (Amanda, not Raggedy) wants a drink of water. She wants to sing me a song she learned in school; not wishing to be gruff and dismissive, I listen. Finally I bid her a THIS-IS-IT good night and return to the kitchen for the ritual tidying-up. The windows are open, letting in some of the first spring air. I feel cozy and content as I put things away, wipe counters, straighten and arrange and shape my home. The drone of the news-radio station is comforting; so is the leftover chocolate cake I sample without guilt.

I decide to sit on the front porch for a few minutes and look at the stars. There are two in the west that must be part of some constellation. They're close together and look like eyes staring down at me. The eyes of God? I am lost in a reverie when a shadow falls across my consciousness. My husband, silhouetted against the brightness, looks out through the screen door. "When are you coming to bed?"

"Soon," I say, trying to conceal my irritation. *I love you, but go away.*

"Well, don't stay up too late. You know how you hate being tired."

I do hate being tired; I don't deal with it well. But sometimes my need for solitude is so powerful, I'm willing to risk fatigue for the gift of time alone. Fifteen, twenty minutes will do. More is better. Time to look at the stars, time to read for pleasure, time to spin dreams and let my mind dance over memories, speculations, even book ideas.

I have to have this. And I don't get it often enough.

There are times I feel my life is as teeming as some Third World marketplace, that the crowd of officemates, the cries of children, even the stream of traffic echo the crush of cyclists, the shouts of vendors hawking fresh fish, the bawling of cattle.

It is then I feel drained and want to go find an undiscovered beach somewhere. Just me and the dolphins and the trade winds. Or I think about a book-lined study, the kind you see in old English movies, with a flickering fire, leather chairs, and one of those wonderful globes that stands on the floor. ("The exploration, Sir Henry, will begin here.")

This longing for solitude is somewhat ironic. There have been times in my life when I've been too much alone—no work and few friends. Back when I had a regular Saturday-night date with Mary Tyler Moore and the gang at the TV station, I longed for what I now have: an interesting, busy life.

But there is a price to pay. I go to the office, someone knocks on the door, the phone chirps, the computer hums. Even the piles of paper insistently clamor: *Do me.* I go home, the TV is on, the phone rings, I am wanted. On such evenings even the sizzle of meat grilling in the pan is irritating, and I feel like escaping to some retreat center where silence is enforced.

When it comes right down to it, lack of solitude is a spiritual issue. There may be great saints who commune with God over the clatter of the computer printer—but I don't know of any. For all my reliance on praying on the wing and practicing the presence as I scrub the kitchen floor, I wonder about God getting crowded out of my life. Working women with families are especially vulnerable (so are mothers of young children). Frankly, I'm a little envious of the women who can sit down with their coffee and their Bible in the morning, still the other voices, and in author Max Lucado's words, "go to the summit" with Christ. When I think about having time alone with God several hours a week, the peak appears inaccessibly distant, ice-bound and wreathed in fog.

How then can we connect?

Realistically, we may need to content ourselves with odd chunks of time carved out. This may be one of those seasons we have to get through. And church can provide that mountaintop experience Lucado talks about.

But I am convinced that God unquestionably uses people—sometimes sends us people—to give us spiritual sustenance as well. Like Amanda, that night she told me she would always be around. Like my

husband, that night I was so in need of comfort. Like
my mentor, that night he told me I should write.

We for whom personal devotional time is often
wishful thinking need to be especially alert to these
opportunities. If our lives are crowded, that may not
always be something to flee, but to walk toward, arms
wide open. Work, and the relationships it brings,
might just bring us closer to God.

Here the paradox asserts itself again. The very
busyness of our lives is a strain. It siphons our energy,
makes us cross, kindles nagging feelings of inadequacy. Yet it is also an unquestionable blessing. To
have family, to have work, to have friends — all illumi-
nated in the light of Christ, to whom we have
surrendered ourselves — these are huge gifts.

Certainly many of our dealings with others are
mundane, having to do with job concerns, chores at
home, idle small talk. Sometimes, though, an encounter can reach deeper; this is when God touches us
gently and says, *I am here. I have not forgotten you. Pay
attention!*

I've already spoken of my friend Charlotte.
Despite the fact that she is tall, slender, and beautiful,
with a cloud of long brown hair, there is a bit of the
earth mother about her. Charlotte is of Hungarian
extraction and I can imagine her saying, "Sit down.
Eat some chicken paprikash and you'll feel better."
Charlotte hugs me when she sees me and always asks
me if there is anything she can do. She tells me she's
praying for my dad in the hospital, and I know she is.
Charlotte has embodied Christ for me — and by so
doing, she makes me want to serve in turn.

Yesterday I had lunch with a book editor. She
and I had worked together on various projects over
the years, but had not seen each other for a while. It
was fun to catch up over French onion soup. We

discussed our common business, mutual friends, prospective authors—then she casually mentioned a possible venture for me, an exciting opportunity. Nothing concrete; my life does not follow the I-prayed-and-the-check-was-in-the-mail story. But she, perhaps quite unknowingly, encouraged me on a day when I was contemplating all sorts of different career directions, wondering how doors could open without my having to bash them down.

God used my editor friend, too. He uses those who express interest in our lives, make us laugh, ask how we are, challenge us, sit quietly with us. His Spirit can flash out in an unexpected hello, a phone call, an animated exchange in a meeting, a compliment from someone who does not give them lightly.

It's not solitude—but it is a nurturing of sorts. It's the rejuvenating sort of companionship, not the wearying, clamorous cast of thousands. Such experiences may not a summit make, but they can form nice little rolling hills—and sometimes, we can see God just as easily as from the peak.

12

When I Grow Up
I Want to Be
Suzie Homemaker

A few days ago my mother-in-law was talking
about how she didn't need to lift the entire top of
her new stove to clean around the burners. "Oh, yes,"
I said. "That's a terrible job." So terrible I never do it.
It made me think, not for the first time: *Maybe I'm not
a very good housekeeper.*

Our windows need washing inside and out. I'm
thinking of paying Amanda, who likes to spray
things, to do them. She's all of six. What does that tell
you? Our refrigerator should probably be cordoned
off with a big blaze-orange warning sign, like Times
Beach, Missouri. I iron not, neither do I mend.

When I get really busy, my house almost seems
to be an unwanted intruder. (Me: "Who are you?"
Deep gravelly voice: "Remember me? I am your
house. I provide warmth, shelter, equity, and a place
to cram your paper piles.")

But if I had the money, would I hire a cleaning
service? I'm not sure. There's something about the idea
of strangers scrubbing my house that's not appealing.

Besides, would they love what they're dusting?

Then I was home alone one day. I'm not ever
alone for any great stretch of time, but this day I had

an entire afternoon to myself. I sat in our living room,
scanning the newspaper. I read recipes. (I have this
pile of food sections I'm saving; my romantically
domestic notion is that I'll actually make Pita Stuffs
and Berry-Cherry Pie someday. Some of the clippings
go back ten years. Haven't used 'em yet.)

I did the dishes and tidied the kitchen, checked
the mail, thumped the barometer. I felt like being
old-fashioned, so I decided to make a casserole for
dinner. After the tan, gloppy stuff was baking away,
I went into the living room and looked at the new
wall unit we recently acquired. I moved the blue
violin and the rainbow-hued vase to the top, where
they'd catch the light. Set a large clear bowl filled
with shells in the center—so! Removed a couple of
less-desirable pieces. Dusted the top of some books.
Stood back, and nodded with satisfaction: Yes.

Then I moved through the other rooms of the
house. A plumped pillow here, a closed curtain there.
I thought of my dear ones, off on their pursuits, and I
had a deep sense of contentment, a feeling of making
a home for them. I set the table with candles and care
(the casserole would be improved by low lighting).
Finally, everything was ready. *I still have it,* I thought.
I can still create a home.

I really liked feeling that way.

But I don't always want to be the person waiting,
the one everyone else comes home to after their ex-
ploits in the great world. It conjures up pictures from
the old "Dick Van Dyke Show"—Mary Tyler Moore
in her Capri slacks, greeting hubby at the door and
saying "Cheese fondue for dinner, hon!" I'd love to
have Mary Tyler Moore's legs—but I don't want to be
Laura Petrie.

Neither do I always want to rush breathlessly
through the door, Burberry trench coat swinging, as I

survey undone breakfast dishes and check my answering machine for messages. No lights on in the house, no warmth emanating from the oven. Yes, my husband does cook dinner sometimes, but—and maybe I am showing my age here—I love cooking for him (he'll eat my casseroles). Every so often I feel good about being the one who welcomes with warmth, who inquires about the day and brings the Coke and slippers.

Men aren't getting enough pampering these days, I suspect. Too many of them are themselves shouldering a big share of domestic and child-care responsibilities. I know households where the husband comes home, exhausted after a hard day and long commute, and the wife, instead of greeting him with gladness, hands him the baby and says, "Here. Your turn." Fifty-fifty. The modern relationship. But there's no care there.

Ten years before Rob and Laura, Doris Day starred in a musical called *Calamity Jane*. I particularly remember one scene where the happy cowgirl who had won her man (Howard Keel) transformed his rude bachelor house into a home. As she arranged wildflowers in vases, dusted with one of those feathery things, hung curtains, and scraped Dakota mud off her man's boots, she gaily sang, "A woman's touch . . ." The message: She may have been the fastest draw west of the Red River, but she was a real woman at heart.

Laugh if you will at the stereotypes, but I think there's something to that. My husband has a good eye for the aesthetic. But I have noticed that when I get through a room, it's clean, really clean; it has a certain glow to it that comes from tender attention. No ServiceMaster team can love my house, can welcome my family.

So while I may never be able to be—or want to be—a full-time homemaker, I relish the opportunities I do have to make my house a home, to pamper my family—as only a woman can. Whether or not I surprise them with a casserole.

13

Thank God It's Sunday

A summer Saturday morning, about eight-thirty. I am
just waking after about ten hours' sleep. Sunshine is
trying to get in past the crack in the window shade. My
husband comes in quietly, bearing gifts. "Good morning,
love! Would you like some coffee?"

After a leisurely peruse through the newspaper, I cook
French toast and sausage for breakfast. Amanda has gotten
up, and we all gather around the table to eat and discuss
what to do on this sunny June day. Will it be strawberry
picking? A hike through the restored prairie? Maybe a visit
to family just across the Wisconsin border? Or a bike ride?

The house is clean, the lawn is mowed, the bills are
up-to-date. My husband has no ministry commitments and
I have completed all my writing projects. Amanda is bored
with cartoons and eager to spend some time in God's open
spaces.

We opt for the strawberry patch and a picnic. When
we arrive at the farm, there are only a few other happy
people a-berrying. The air is cool and all the bugs have gone
somewhere else. We load our baskets with the succulent
little rubies. They taste as good as they look.

Later, I make strawberry shortcake and Devonshire
cream. We eat supper on our backyard picnic table and

admire the roses now bursting into bloom. A Baltimore oriole whistles from a nearby tree.

The next day, the Lord's day, we are up in plenty of time to get to church. My husband and I read the Bible and pray together to get the day started off right. All Amanda's good clothes are clean and ironed and none of her tights have holes. We have laid out clothes, Bible, offering the night before. We arrive at church early and stroll in smiling.

The truth:

My husband has a 7:30 A.M. basketball game, so I get up early with him. As I do every day of the week. I get out my to-do list pad (the first item on every page reads "Find the list"). I can see the dust settling on the furniture like sediment. We talk over the day's events. Will it be five loads of laundry today or a jaunt to Kmart for new shoes for Amanda, whose Sunday shoes are so tight you can see the outline of her toes? He has to drive twenty-five miles this afternoon on business, so the grass won't get cut; anyway, it looks like rain. My daughter runs out and turns on some noisy cartoon. Why do all the commercials for kids feature rap? She eats a frozen waffle in front of the set and doesn't get dressed until eleven.

The television blares, the washer agitates, the birds squawk to be fed. I worry about finishing work due next week. At the end of the day, we eat frozen pizza in the kitchen. In between, the house has somehow been cleaned, the writing half-done (as I periodically run outside to arbitrate disputes between Amanda and her playmates). The lawn still needs mowing. We are all exhausted and go to bed early.

Somewhere I read that people today are so busy during the weekend that they look forward to going back to work — the "TGIM" syndrome. With so many

women working outside the home, Saturdays become
a day crammed with everything that doesn't get done
on weekdays: housecleaning, laundry, yard work,
grocery shopping. Then there's soccer practice and
kids' birthday parties and Scout campouts and visits
to Grandma's and doctor's appointments. Perhaps
there's a work deadline to be met that requires some
weekend hours at the computer. After all this, returning to the office feels like a recreational break. And
you don't get paid for weekend chores when you're
grown up.

I have a confession to make: Occasionally the
pace becomes so hectic that my husband and I come
to Sunday morning and say, "Let's not go to church."
Every couple of months or so we decide to give ourselves
a morning with Charles Kuralt, the Sunday paper,
and no pressure. We naturally do this with mixed
feelings — but it affords us a whole day of leisure.

But it isn't an ideal solution. We love our church;
our occasional lack of attendance leaves us with a
peculiarly empty space in the week. It feels wrong,
like starting a sentence without a capital letter.

So should I make my Saturdays less beaver-like?
I'm beginning to think housework itself is a form of
relaxation, a no-brain effort that gives me a break
from my usual mental intensity. Perhaps I could
order my Saturdays so half my day is spent on chores
and the other half left free for "fun" (something I
vaguely remember having back around 1976). Or
perhaps I could cram more into my weeknights to
free up Saturday time.

But the real secret to redeeming the weekend
may lie in the way we approach our Sundays.

I once interviewed a number of men and women
on how they handle Sundays. Many admitted, "I

don't think we *do* handle it." Church all morning,
afternoon naps, shopping, more chores. I was surprised by the number of Christians who said, "Look,
you have to be realistic about this. Work has to get
done somehow." They don't feel good about violating
the commandment, but neither do they want to revert
to a legalism of bygone days: Don't go to movies,
don't play ball, don't read anything save God's Word.
If it rains on Saturday, you have to mow the lawn
Sunday afternoon.

The Sunday of leisure described above is rare for
us. But the truth is, when we do Sunday right, I love
it. I like to get up in time to read the color comics—
"Annie" and "Winnie Winkle" and "Cathy." If I am
up early enough, I can leaf through the entire newspaper. My husband plays Gaither hymns or a Bach
chorale to get us in the mood. We have our usual mad
dash to church (that seems to be a given; we could get
up at five and still have a mad dash). But once there,
we settle into our seats and take a deep breath, glad to
go into the house of the Lord once again. Friends
smile at us. We might sing a great old favorite like
"To God Be the Glory" or "A Mighty Fortress"—in
either case, I know all the verses by heart. The
prayers, the special music, the sermon, times of silence and times of sharing—all work their way into
my soul. Surely the Lord is in this place.

Coffee time, children's Sunday school, adult
study, small groups; kids running around on the
grass after church and long conversations in the
narthex. We are always among the last to leave unless
we have other commitments; we love the lingering,
the visiting. This is how church should feel. Why be
in such a hurry to escape God's house?

If I let it, church can seem like just another obligation—like work. But it is not, not really. Church is me

before God. Just me as his child: not the careerperson, not the parent, not the spouse, not the tightrope walker doing her high-wire act. I really need church, and I am learning to open my mind to what the pastor has for me in his sermon (it helps to take notes), pay attention to the words of the hymns, bring my honest needs to our small group.

If we can, we resist too many Sunday-afternoon commitments. Our frenzied Saturdays pay off in a slower Sabbath pace. I snooze or read or play with my daughter. The three of us often take long walks. Usually I'll spend time cooking a special dinner (preferably something like a roast that guarantees weeknight leftovers).

And thus the rhythm is set.

Our bodies and spirits need these comforting cycles of work and rest, frenzy and reflection, repetitious chores and renewing worship. When we move too far away from them, something in the biochemistry of our souls can go awry.

My Saturday in the berry patch may be a distant dream. But my Sunday isn't. And that, as much as anything, may help my Mondays.

14

Giving My Child
a Summer

I remember summer.
When I was a child, summer lasted forever. We
lived in an area of open meadows dotted with wild
petunias, black-eyed Susans, buttercups, and daisies. I
would hide in the tall grass and listen to the breeze
sigh through the reeds. When the grass went to seed, I
would pretend the flowers were wheat and try to
make cereal. Hot afternoons found my friends and me
wading in the creek and chasing dragonflies; during
long evenings we would play Mother May I and
Statue-Maker and Red Light, Green Light until it got
dark and our parents yelled for us to come in.

Summer was bare feet, fireflies, freedom. Even
the dogs ran loose. Summer was my mother fixing
breakfast for us in her robe after Dad went off to
work.

Yes, we had day camp, swimming lessons, Vacation Bible School. But mostly I remember time—and
more time.

It's different now. Soon my daughter will be in
first grade, at school all day. I wonder, *Has she had
enough summer? Has she had enough time to run footloose
through the neighborhood, playing and chasing the ice-cream*

truck? How will Amanda remember her summers —
and her mother's role in giving her what should be a
season of golden freedom?

Summer can be tough for working mothers who
often have to cobble together an arrangement of
babysitters, church activities, camp, and other programs to occupy their children and set their minds at
rest. Those who can may change their work hours.
Others, like one woman I know, simply cut back — to
their family's financial detriment. And sometimes,
unavoidably, children are left on their own.

So it isn't the same, not like when I could burst
into our kitchen and shout, "Mom! Can I have a
lemonade stand?" — and there she'd be.

Nevertheless . . . I do the best I can.

For example, I remember a rainy day this summer. I happened to be home that day, so Amanda and
I went for a morning walk to the local playground.
Suddenly a shower came up, and as distant thunder
cracked, we ran back home hand-in-hand, laughing
and getting soaked. When it was time for lunch, I set
up a picnic on our screened porch, with a red-and-
white checked tablecloth and bright plastic picnic
ware. We sat and ate sandwiches and fruit while the
rain drummed down on the porch roof. We agreed
that the rain was good for the flowers and that we
could see the grass turning green. After a time, the
showers ended and we went back outside. Amanda
jumped barefoot in the puddles.

It's nice to slow the summer pace. When I don't
absolutely have to be working, my time is Amanda's.
Usually what we do together is simple. She shows me
a tree loaded with mulberries, and we eat them and
laugh at each other's purple lips. I buy her ice cream
from the local Good Humor Man, and we lie in the
grass and look for four-leaf clovers (and sometimes

find them). I sit on the front porch while she runs off to play with a friend in their shared "hideout" in the bushes.

We do amusement parks, museums, various church activities. But I think my child enjoys most the roaming, the running. She, like her mother, would play outdoors until the stars spangled the east if a responsible party didn't round her up and drag her grimy sleepyhead home for bathtime and maybe a dish of sherbet before bed.

Just like my mom did.

I remember summer—and I remember being six and how it felt. I want to give my child some of that same sense of spaciousness, of timelessness. Soon enough she will be off to school, sitting in a real classroom, wearing new shoes and having to be quiet. The fireflies will die and the days will grow short, and the pail and shovel she digs mud with will lie forgotten under the evergreens. I want my child to have a summer—because summer is for kids.

I look at her now. My, she looks tanned and healthy! She has lived in shorts and sundresses and sandals, but the time is coming when new jeans and sneakers will be the order of the day.

She says now, "Mommy, are you done working?" She is used to Mom going to the office or writing in the bedroom. And often enough that's okay with her; peers are so much more interesting than parents. But there are times—like now—when Mom *is* done working, when Mom is all hers.

"Can I have a popsicle?" she asks.

"Sure," I say. "Maybe I'll have one too. I always liked the blue ones."

15

But What Are You Saving Time For?

My husband and I like to order food from Market Day, a fund-raising enterprise that enables us to buy large quantities of items like chicken breasts, frozen fruit, and mini-pizzas. It's good stuff, and it helps the PTA at our local school. But the other day, as we looked over the order form, Fritz said, "Here, let's get these microwave pancakes! Already made!"

I looked at him. "*What?* It takes ten minutes to stir up batter and pour it on the griddle."

We ordered the pancakes and they were so-so. Certainly they cooked (is that the word? Things don't exactly cook in the microwave, they . . . process) into perfect golden circles, in contrast to my hotcakes, which tend to fall into shapes resembling the state of West Virginia, with unappetizing brown speckles on them. But at least mine are the product of honest toil. Eating these processed golden discs felt like a capitulation to the current mania for time management.

That same week, a magazine editor asked me to write a fifteen-hundred-word article. Fifteen hundred words is not a lot—about three pages, maybe four if you throw in a large illustration. It's the perfect length for today's busy woman who wants her information in McNugget-sized bites. Because she has no time.

Maybe. One of the never-ending irritants of my life is the Tyranny of the Schedule, of having to plan everything down to quarter-hour segments. A working mother quickly learns how to mentally back everything up: *If I leave for the office by 8:30 in the morning, I have to be up by 6 in order to shower, shampoo, skim the paper, tidy the house, scarf down a bowl of fiber, get the kids dressed and off to school.* (One book I read said that the working woman should get up an hour before everyone else. My husband rises at 5:30. Forget it.) And always allow for contingencies: a run in the nylons (paw through the drawer for a pair that only has a hole in the toe), a balky child, misplaced homework, an inconvenient phone call ("this is the bank . . ."). Then reverse everything at night so you're in bed by 10 P.M.

I hate this.

I'm not organized by nature; I've had to learn how to be. If it were up to me, I would happily drift through my day. Oh, everything would get done eventually—but on my terms. When I have a free day—not Sunday-with-church, not Saturday-with-chores, not holidays-with-relatives—just unscheduled, delicious TIME—my entire system opens up and breathes. I actually consult recipes, start dinner at four, and clean up as I go. I can take a nap, talk to my child, write a letter. (It's no coincidence that the last time I really corresponded with people was when I was unmarried, unemployed, and obviously childless.)

The very sensation of having time makes me realize how forward-moving we are forced to be. But really it's a question both of lack of time and compulsive time management. Yes, those of us who work outside the home have fewer hours to spend inside the home (or doing anything else). So anything that helps us simplify our lives is welcome—although I'm not sure about microwave pancakes.

But this is what I worry about: Saving time can become an end in itself, not a means to a more satisfying life. We don't know how to live any other way, so we become miserly with our minutes. Meals are gulped; so are chapters in books. We zap restlessly from one television channel to the next; we drive everywhere and drum our fingers impatiently in the drive-up bank line when two cars wait ahead of us. We even rush our children: bathstorybed, another time slot, there! That's over! Hurrying can become an addiction.

And we resist those things that seem to take too much time. Long sermons. Walking instead of driving. Hanging out the laundry. I recently read that cats—not dogs—are now the most popular pet in America. Dogs belong to an earlier era of big families and open spaces and women at home; cats are perfect for our era of childless households and high-rise living, or so the *USA Today* sort of wisdom goes. How sad when we're too busy to let ourselves be loved by a pet.

Some of this may have a historical inevitability. Turn-of-the-century writers complained about the accelerated pace of the Machine Age; sometimes I wonder if the advent of computers and fax machines and satellite communication hasn't altered our perception of time in some fundamental biochemical way. If we were to land in, say, Colonial America circa preacher Jonathan Edwards' time, would we be amazed at how slowly people moved and spoke—how long everything took?

Yet we're never going to return to an eighteenth-century pace. Still, something is awry when people

say sleep is an attractive-but-quaint artifact of our
agrarian past. If our lives are so hectic that we be-
grudge our bodies seven hours' sleep, we're too busy.
And what are we doing with that extra couple of
hours? If we were reading the complete works of
Dickens or planting an orchard, I'd say hooray! But
my guess is, we're filling those insomniac minutes
with more compulsion—read another report, throw
another load of laundry into the wash—or more
television—who's on "Letterman" tonight?

So what is time for?

Time, like everything else, comes from God. His
very first act of Creation was to separate day from
night. There was evening and there was morning.
Time is a gift to be held tenderly and used wisely to
his glory. Savor this phrase: *the fullness of time.* Fullness,
roundness, generosity. Not hurried stinginess, not
self-centered convenience, not insectlike scurrying.

Save time where you must to enjoy it where you
will. Certainly there's no inherent virtue in laboring
long over everything as our forebears did. I know: I
don't have a dishwasher, and I wish I did. I would
rather spend time with my daughter than wash and
stack dishes.

But every now and then I love *not* saving time. I
love expending hours on something that cannot be
done any other way, like tending a vegetable garden.
You can't rush the process. The soil has to be roto-
tilled, fertilized, prepared just so; the rows have to be
hoed straight and true; the seeds placed, not thrown,
the correct distance apart. There are vagaries of
drought and heat, wind and storm, to contend with.
But gardens won't be hurried or controlled—and
that's rather nice.

There's no way to read a novel fast, either. When
I was a child, I spent many a summer afternoon lying

on our porch swing, a stack of books at hand. I would creak and read, creak and read, and the world would disappear as I rambled in the Avonlea meadows with Anne of Green Gables or kept vigil with Jo March over her consumptive sister Beth.

Lazy summer afternoons are a luxury I no longer have. But recently I did stay up too late to read an engrossing novel by a complex Christian author. I *should* have gone to bed. I *should* have kept the schedule. But I read hundreds of pages for hours in the quiet—and it felt like the fullness of time.

So, a bit like the book-reading child I was once, I don't always push myself. Despite the constant demands on my time, I sometimes resist the pressure to organize everything. It may be my little gesture of rebellion against the Schedule Dictator, but I don't always compulsively track how long it takes to do something and what I have to do next. I don't even wear a watch.

Maybe it all comes down to the tension between two things-at-once: some juggling, some space. Some sending of faxes, some rolling out of pie crust dough. With lard, please. And in a real oven. Not the microwave.

16

Give It to Me Leaded

I lie awake, listening to the last crickets chirping outside the window. Cold has slowed their singing. The calendar may cling to summer, but the crickets know better. I shiver contentedly and burrow deeper under the quilts.

But to no avail; sleep has fled like summer fled the Midwest last weekend. I peer at the digital clock: 4:40 A.M. Too much to think about. This will be a flat-out day — company luncheon, marathon meeting, long-overdue hair appointment (when my hair starts curling over my ears like some frowzy bird, it's code blue time), women's potluck at church tonight. Of course I haven't made anything. Maybe there are some strawberries in the refrigerator I could scrape the mold from. A delightful taste treat. They want me to give a reading; I hope my voice doesn't betray me by quavering as it sometimes does when I speak before a group.

Worked until six last night, putting in overtime in preparation for an out-of-town trip and an afternoon jaunt to the circus with my daughter. It's all she's been talking about. This is my life, taking from one hand to give to the other. Nothing is won without surrendering something else.

This is ridiculous. I can't keep lying here, my
mind running in futile circles. Maybe I'm achieving a
new level of diminished sleep need. Wouldn't that be
nice — sleep about five hours a night, pack two lives
into one day, and still look daisy-fresh?

Oh, well. I get up, almost angry at my husband
for his ability to sleep through anything. A garbage
truck could grind away in our front yard and Fritz
would not wake up.

We need to get one of those coffeemakers with a
timer you can set so we can wake to the fragrance of
the noble brew. Such hardship to wait ten minutes.
I'm considering buying Fritz a sleek new Krups for
our anniversary. I mean, we need one; we're still
using an old Dial-a-Brew. I pour the water through
and remember the old Danny Thomas commercials.
Or was it Joe DiMaggio?

The machine starts bumping and hissing. Here it
comes. I know I'm not supposed to like this stuff —
strong, dark, high-test. I've read that coffee
consumption peaked around 1962 and has been
plummeting ever since. People are drinking soda pop
now, even for breakfast. Soda pop? That sweet fizzy
gunk? How do people get moving in the morning? To
me these statistics reflect our nation's slow slide into
moral turpitude. When coffee was king, people lived
in cold sturdy places like Fargo and Buffalo and
walked to work at the local mill after breakfasting on
hash browns and three fried eggs. Coffee does something to the fiber of the soul. Garrison Keillor's Lake
Wobegonians consume gallons of the stuff, and *they're*
good, solid Middle Americans.

There. The bubbling has stopped. I lovingly select
a mug and pour. It feels almost sacramental, this
drinking of the first cup. Franky Schaeffer has written
that "breakfast is God's" (along with everything else).

I like that idea. And I like the idea that God created the coffee plant, which grows on lush, breezy hillsides in nice places like Costa Rica. Where does Diet Slice grow? In a lab somewhere.

Now I'm drinking and fully awake, ready to hit the day running. The news-radio station is predicting rain, which makes me happy—I love crummy weather. Amanda will need to wear her raincoat, which is probably too short. All of a sudden she's outgrowing everything. The other day I tried a dress on her that fit last spring and her knees and wrists stuck out of it like some lanky, rawboned country boy who hardly fits in the back desk of the one-room schoolhouse. When did she grow to be so tall? While I was at a meeting somewhere?

Coffee helps you think, clarify, plan. Coffee is rational, coffee is grownup. I drank my first cup at college, and it felt like a rite of passage, like wearing pantyhose for the first time. I think our society needs more of these rites of passage, a sharper divide between adolescence and adulthood. Everything's too blurred now—kids who look like Madonna, forty year olds who think they're still eighteen.

Coffee (make it leaded, please) is also the fuel that powers women like me. A few slugs and zap! Ready to take on the world (or face myself in the mirror, which on some days amounts to the same thing). Coffee in the car on the way to work (and if anyone has found a commuter mug that doesn't leak or spill, please contact me care of this publisher). Coffee at the office, even though the machine never gets cleaned and the stuff tastes like stormwater runoff. Coffee at meetings. Coffee at church—and that raises a question: What do fizz-drinkers do when they socialize after worship? Hold a placebo Styrofoam cup in their hands so they fit in?

Now the coffee is cooling. I page through the newspaper, but my mind is elsewhere. My daughter's library book is overdue. I should really be taking a walk instead of sitting here feeding my oral fixation. I need to read some manuscripts in preparation for the editorial meeting today. Or should I join my husband, now up and about, for prayer?

Perhaps I can do it all. If you ask me, I can do anything. I am Woman, hear me drink!

17

Why You Can't Get It All Done, and Why It's Okay

*L*ast Saturday we helped our friends rake bushels of leaves from their hilly yard. She was pregnant, he was overworked, we needed the exercise, and their village permits leaf burning—wonderful, fragrant, nostalgic, environmentally unsound leaf burning. After a homemade bread-and-soup lunch, I milled around the kitchen watching them clean up. I noticed a small box of nuts on the counter.

"Isn't that last year's Christmas gift from our employer?" I asked with amusement.

My friend laughed. "Yes! I keep meaning to get rid of it. It's been there for months, and we'll never eat them. It's sort of my symbol of futility."

Another woman I know has mini-blinds. She says she hasn't cleaned them in two years. Jane's blinds are her symbol of things undone—futility.

I don't know what my badge of dishonor is, my visual reminder of neglect. Could it be the rotting pumpkins that sat on our front step till almost Thanksgiving? The wrinkled paisley skirt I never ironed and now will never wear because it's too big and too baggy for today's fashions? Or the unsent birthday cards?

I try to keep up. I really do. But sometimes I feel like I'm one step ahead of chaos, one day away from having putrefying pumpkins slide down the front steps. And now there's a new threat to the fragile equilibrium I've created: our obligation, as concerned parents, to participate as full partners in our daughter's education. We can't let the Japanese and Germans and Koreans overtake our children—so we are deluged almost daily with paper from Amanda's school. Homework, which of course we have to help her with. Stories to help her write. Things to sign. "Suggested" at-home exercises to work on. So much stuff to read that the very trees themselves cry out at the waste of paper.

It's all too much. Yet . . . you can't blow off these school obligations. If the skirt doesn't get ironed, if the drawer doesn't get cleaned out, no one will suffer. But I have to help my daughter keep up in school. I don't want the teachers to think I'm one of those negligent working moms whose kids have to make an appointment to spend time with them. Besides, she's a bright child and an eager learner. It's a joy to see the light bulbs going off in her six-year-old head.

So I help assemble foil and cookie sprinkles and raisins to decorate her cardboard turkey (which is late). I read reams of bulletins from the principal. I practice penmanship with her (which is ironic; my handwriting is terrible). And I guess some of it sinks in.

Sometimes, though, I feel as if I cannot think about one more thing, that every nook and cranny of my brain is jammed full, like an overstuffed luggage compartment on an airplane. I think it's a question of mental and emotional depletion. For those of us coping with so many demands, this kind of depletion is a hidden stressor. We know the toll physical fatigue can take, but brains—and spirits—get tired too. I know I'm over the edge when I make stupid mistakes, cry, snap at my husband. When I neglect not only the insignificant (the pumpkins) but the important (a few nights ago a friend told me, "It seems like I always call you and you don't call me").

We cannot throw off these obligations unless we decide to chuck it all and live off roots and berries. But the truth of the matter is, just as too many of us are under the thumb of Day-Timer Tyranny, too many of us are ruled by unrealistic expectations of how much we "should" get done and how much energy we "should" have. Abetted by media images of women executives who live on four hours' sleep and cross time zones like you or I walk from the stove to the sink, we think we should be bionic.

But we all have different capacities. I know one woman who says she probably does best on about ten hours of sleep and arranges her life accordingly. Another acquaintance admits he can "go all the time." He is one of those wondrous people who doesn't need much sleep, who's up at five singing "Feelings" in the shower (to the disgust of his wife, who peaks around noon and goes downhill from there).

It's hard enough to work full or part time and care for a family. (Even as I am sitting here writing this, my daughter is banging on the door.) We are doing well, very well, just to manage those two challenges day in, day out.

The danger of discouragement — literally, "disheartenment" — is that we can become spiritually enervated. Not suffering servants, shriveled servants. We open ourselves up to the whispers of the Liar: *You are a failure. You will never be good enough. Why even try?*

When I feel like this, I need help. Most of us working women are so used to relying on our own resources, our own get-up-and-go, that we can forget

the meaning of letting go and clinging to the One who
is there—even though he may seem busy elsewhere.

How did Jesus know, two millennia ago when he
called the heavy-laden to come unto him, that in 1991
there would be a fortyish woman in a midwestern
town who needs his message so desperately? Who
seeks his rest so intensely?

He knew. He still knows, and he cares, and I'm
learning that he alone can make me feel good about
myself, give me rest, nourish my spirit. Through the
tears and exhaustion he comes; through a romp with
a child he comes; through the benison of a good
night's sleep he comes; through the invitation of a
friend to "come over and talk" he comes.

He also comes when I practice his presence—
when I fling prayers to him throughout my day, when
I try simply to be aware of his gifts to me, when I
stand still (not often enough, believe me) and enjoy
his creation.

This is what we need to remember: God created
us as limited human beings. We are not gods, endlessly self-sufficient, boundlessly talented. There is no
sin in acknowledging we cannot do it all. And—
paradox again—there is a joyful freedom when we do
assert our limitations, and learn to laugh about the
nuts on the counter, the skirt balled up in the clothes
basket. There's liberation when we can say without
guilt, "I need to take a nap."

Speaking of which, that doesn't sound like such a
bad idea.

18

Let's Keep in Touch—Really

*H*ooray! A friend has come back into my life!
This almost never happens. People move out of
state, change jobs or churches, or simply drift away.
You promise each other you'll write, call, visit on
vacations—and for a time, you make the effort. But
eventually the commitment wanes and a once-vibrant
relationship withers to a quick note jotted on a Christmas card.

Lately I've said, or cried, good-bye to my share of
dear ones. Redheaded Randy and his wife Jeron—
their dimpled Annalyn was Amanda's "bestest"
friend. Virginia—the sort of warm extrovert that
draws shy people like me because they do most of the
talking and we can listen in silent happiness. Scott,
my former boss. Sharon, a confidante and prayer
partner.

We sporadically keep in touch, but we all have
too many immediate claims on our time. New friends
move in to assume the places of the old—but do they,
really? The loss of a friend, whether through neglect
or life's turnings, leaves a gap that never quite fills. I
can't replace a friend like I can a broken piece of my
Blue Danube china. If it were up to me, no one would

ever leave; old friends would be joined by new and
we would all live happily ever after.

So when Ruth and I picked up the threads, I was
amazed and delighted. She and I had worked together several years ago. Now, quite unexpectedly,
our stories again intersected.

We sat in the corner booth of the Sizzler for a long
catch-up lunch. Cold rain streamed down the windows
as we talked about what God was doing in our lives.
Four years—an entire presidential term—had elapsed
since we'd parted. We had each added a few lines of
living on our faces; we had each bought a house in the
same neighborhood; we had each launched our children
on new adventures—hers to college, mine to first grade.

I looked at Ruth and realized how much I appreciated the woman she had become in those four years.
I sensed in her a deepening, an intensity born of
internal struggles. We stood poised on the cusp of
new seasons in our lives—she, returning to an office
full time and preparing to marry off a daughter; I,
feeling the tug to write, write, write. We had much to
share with each other, and before we knew it, the
lunch hour had passed.

As we parted, Ruth said, "This has been fun.
Let's stay in touch."

I knew what she meant. It is so frighteningly easy
to get *out* of touch—even when you work down the
hall or live a few blocks away. Tending friendships
takes a good chunk of time and energy, two com-
modities in short supply for most of us. We are
reluctant to "bother" other people. Several times I
have picked up the phone, even started to dial, then
hung up thinking, *I better not. She's probably busy with
the kids. I hate to intrude.*

But one of the truest pleasures of work is the
companionship it provides, the fascinating kindred

spirits it brings into your life. When professional paths cross regularly, these relationships are easier to maintain. Yet they also can be freighted with the baggage of envy, competitiveness, calculated networking. If a friend calls me to share news of a professional success, I rejoice sincerely — but the worm is in there, burrowing. So my joy is shaded with, *Why can't it be me?*

Working women can lead very crowded, very lonely lives — many acquaintances, few real friends. The office banter and camaraderie can mask a deeper hunger to reach out and *know* another human being — and be known in turn. Sometimes, when the pressures have us down and we are most vulnerable, we may revert to a high-school sense that everyone else is "popular" except us. And we can't go home and dump all this longing on our spouse, who has his own concerns to deal with.

Yet if I sometimes feel isolated and needy, I must share culpability. As I write this, I am gnawed by guilt over several friends I should call — right now. People have moved out of state, and I have not answered their letters. I say I am a person who values loyalty and affection; I do not always act like it.

Yes, some friendships are transitory; some connections are temporary. Let the warmth die and move on. But a good friend is so hard to find that he or she is worth holding onto. And, as a woman who recently moved noted in a letter, "We've forgotten how much energy it takes to make new friends."

Especially for the two-headed woman. But good friends can cut through that tension of too-much-to-do-and-be. I need the nurture — and fun — friends provide. I need people in my life who don't want anything from me except *me*. People I don't have to perform for, who know me too well to be fooled by

my slick attempts to impress. I need people to have a
good time with.

And, on a deeper level. I need friends to hold me
spiritually accountable, people who give me a place to
pray. I used to work with Sharon, my spiritual buddy.
I could walk into her office and vent: "Look, I'm
angry about something that just happened. So-and-so
really dropped the ball on this one. Could we pray
together RIGHT NOW?"

Sharon would. And I would do the same for her.

Because they accept you for who you are, dear
friends can also lovingly let you know when you're
straying off course. Because you respect them, you
don't feel as if you're being hounded by some sort of
Christian KGB. For example, I have another friend
who helps keep my pride reined in. She challenges
me on whom I'm trying to please. But she doesn't
lecture. When she talks about herself, her struggles in
those arenas, I see myself and love her for her
empathetic way of challenging me.

I wish I could have a standing weeknight commitment to be with this friend, to sprawl on her sofa and talk.
Her children are grown and gone; her house is quiet. It
would be a much-needed relief for me. But I feel guilty
about leaving my family at night when I'm not home all
day. So my daughter has mom's attention—but my
friendships fend for themselves. I can't go to my friend's
and eat corn chips and salsa and speak passionately about
those spiritual issues that drive to the marrow of my soul.

Sometimes I wonder if our current emphasis on
family-first is a little overdone. *Do* we fall into near-
idolatry when we elevate the nuclear family above all
other earthly relationships? Is a good friendship such
a poor second choice by comparison?

You can't get into and out of the apostle Paul's
letters without realizing his deep connections to his

friends and fellow builders of the church: "Every day I thank God for you." Priscilla and Aquila and Timothy and the rest *were* his family; my guess is, thoughts of them kept him going through prison and shipwreck and arduous journeys throughout Asia Minor. And he did more than think. He worked at staying in touch.

Likewise, Scripture doesn't say a lot about Jesus' family. What we do see is Jesus and Peter, Jesus and Lazarus, Jesus and Mary Magdalene, Jesus and Mary and Martha, Jesus and the Beloved Disciple. Followers of the Master, yes — but friends and boon companions, too.

Friendship is not a luxury, a nice but expendable extra. For the Christian, it's a biblical necessity. For the woman with two heads, friendship is a sanity preserver.

Back to Ruth. When she and I sat in the Sizzler while the rain coursed down outside, we talked a lot about feeling divided, about the conflicts between choices. She understood me. I understood her. We helped each other that day, I think.

And, God willing, I won't be too busy to keep helping her — to keep in touch.

19

Nesting and Soaring

T his really bothered me. I glanced at our front
door and saw a bunch of Indian corn hanging
from a nail instead of a flowery wreath. "When did
that get up there?" I asked Fritz.

"Three days ago."

This is how out of touch I can get with my own
house. Where was I when it had changed? Busy,
preoccupied, going from the back door to the car to
work and back again? I've hardly used the front door.

Yet, I like my things. I like noticing them and
caring for them. I want to be the one who, observing
the onset of autumn, digs out the Indian corn and
puts it up. Sure, I appreciate my husband's taking the
time to do it, but somehow, it feels wrong.

A woman's house—from the foundation to the I-
beams to the Indian corn on the door—is part of who
she is. Some women are so busy in their careers that
they choose a purely functional lifestyle; they live in
small, sparely furnished condos that are merely
places to sleep. Efficient, pragmatic, empty.

But not me. I complain a lot about my house, but
I dearly love my cozy nest at the corner of Webster
and Forest, with its purple petunias out front, the

swing set in back, the chair rail in the dining room, the set of fairy tales in the bedroom bookcase. I chose the pale-yellow living room paint (but let my husband oversee the painters!). I picked out the ash tree we planted out front. I could spend hours and hours here; my idea of the ideal vacation is two weeks at home catching up.

I like enjoying my house, feeling a kinship with women over the generations. The first radical feminists went wrong in insisting everything had to change, that women had to leave the home in droves and deny this special feminine attribute. Many of us are now seeking to restore the balance; we've proven we can succeed in the work world—but what parts of ourselves have we neglected in the process?

I absolutely need the recharging that comes from caring for my things, from the dusting of my favorite blue-and-white vase—a gift from my sister—to the digging around in my kitchen drawers for egg beaters and rolling pins and pastry blenders when I bake a pie. And when I go too long without doing these things, I begin to feel homesick, out of kilter, oddly lonesome. I need my home to feel anchored in—and I feel like my house misses me when I neglect it.

I hear that the family dinner is in danger of dying out, that no one cooks any more. I hope that's not true. The image of a harried career woman picking up fast food on her way home from the office and dumping it in front of her family is troublesome. Home is where you should feel rejuvenated, rooted. It should be a place where you can rediscover the deepest parts of yourself. Sometimes, I love to sit on the floor and dust my books, one by one. It makes me start feeling like the "me" I've been forever, the "me" that predates career, marriage, and mothering. It takes me back to when I was four and used to sit on my bedroom rug reading the Little Golden Books I kept in a drawer at the bottom of my closet.

I don't travel on business very often, but when I do I'm aware of the artificiality of it all—from the flight attendant's industrial-strength blush to the air-conditioned limo to the synthetic, flame-retardant hotel furniture. It's a distorted environment, cut off from the weather and nature and things that root you in who you are. I wonder about the effect of constant travel on women whose jobs require they pile up bonus points. Does it become harder to hear the chirp of a bird, to read the clouds, to sniff the perfume from a ripe peach?

This, again, is the paradox: To do what I want to do, what I feel called to do, I sometimes have to go away, whether it's to an office or on a business trip or just closeting myself with the computer, writing at home. It's the pull between the poles: I could not give up what I do for the sake of being rooted; a part of me needs to fly.

But I need my nest to come back to. I love to sit in my house, writing, and look out the window. It is fall now, and I can see warblers flitting about in the evergreens, peeping and elusive, on their way south.

And I think of another flock of birds I saw a few days ago. A front from the north had swept in, pushing wind-driven clouds ahead of it. The air was so bracingly fresh it almost seemed to call: *Come away, come away!* I looked up and saw, so high, a covey of nighthawks heading southwest. Something about the instant—the wind, the tiny birds etched against a billowing cloud, the slant of the light—sighed of longing, sadness, change, the urge to soar. I watched until the birds had disappeared somewhere over the curve of the earth. Something—not the cold—made me shiver. *Go,* the moment murmured. *Rise, seek. Let Boreas, the great north wind, drive you forward.*

Well, it was just a moment. I returned to six o'clock and what's for dinner and looking down at the sidewalk so I wouldn't trip. But as I think of those wheeling nighthawks, I remember the Indian corn. To stay, to fly. To remain, to go. To build a nest, to boldly venture. Both are encoded in the birds; the nighthawks will return to this place next April or May. They come back to the same rooftops, the same few square blocks, year in, year out.

So I have to come back to this place, this dear corner. Like the birds, I can both soar and nest. Unlike them, I can both dream and dust—often, at the same time.

20

Woman Flees
Perfection Police

I thought I would fall out of my chair in shock.
This is what my friend Jan was saying: "I always
feel as though I'm inadequate, and everyone else has
it all together."

Jan? Jan runs a successful consulting business, writes
magazine articles, and is working on her first book. She is
thin. She and her husband have a beautifully decorated
house. With her flexible schedule she is able to devote a
lot of time to her young daughter. She is always immacu-
lately groomed. Jan even knows how to tie a scarf. Next
to Jan, I feel like a shambling excuse for a human being.

And *Jan* feels inadequate? I laughed and said, "Jan,
if YOU feel that way, what hope is there for the rest of us?"

I knew Jan was being candid. I respected her for
her honesty, which probably cost her something.

But other women I know have privately confessed the same thing to me. Working women feel
inferior to those who seem to have more lucrative/
fulfilling/prestigious jobs. At-home moms feel inferior to working moms. And most of us wonder if our
children, houses, marriages, spiritual conditions
measure up.

To what? To whom?

Women today are under grinding pressure to be
perfect. Looks matter—a lot. Surfaces count. We're
sup-posed to want to make money, be successful,
have ambition. I once read about a woman CEO who
has her own private exercise room next to her office.
"No time is no excuse!" the article chided. The Perfection Police are out there, and they're gonna get you.
No excuses! Shape up!

But where does this pressure come from? The
media? To an extent, yes. Everyone on television is
perfect (except Roseanne, and who wants to be like her?).
No one is old, handicapped, ugly, or poor; everyone
is professional, upper-middle class, and generally
white. Although externally we may reject these images, they worm their way into our psyches and
become the yardstick by which we measure ourselves.

But the canker is also in us. In me. I do judge
others by their appearance. When I entertain, I bustle
about, polishing and waxing and scrubbing and
stuffing clutter under beds—so people will be impressed. I want to be admired; I want others to
marvel, "How does she do it?" I am selective about
my struggles. I share problems I have answers for. I
enjoy being seen with the important, the well known.

And sometimes I feel like I'm lying—just to keep
up appearances.

One of my favorite old gospel hymns is "Victory
in Jesus." We have a record of George Beverly Shea
songs, and I love the rollicking trumpet arrangement:
"Oh, victory in Jesus / My Savior forever! / He
sought me, and bought me / With his redeeming
blood . . ." When my spirits flag and I need a reminder of what God has done for me—for all who call
upon his name—Bev's music is a bracing tonic. Yet I
wonder if we don't take this "victorious living" idea
too far. It isn't just the media with their glamorous,

guilt-inducing images. We, good Christian women, are doing it to ourselves.

We can misinterpret the "new life in Christ" to mean that now we and others should be problem-free. And when we fall short, we feel alone in our inadequacy. At our meeting, Jan, whom I consider one of the most put-together women on God's green earth, confessed, "I think I'm the only one who feels this way."

Jan, dear sister, you're not! Here each of us is, secretly blundering through life, looking over our shoulder to see if anyone saw us snag our stockings or caught us eating ice cream straight out of the carton. To see if some invisible host of judgment is monitoring our mistakes.

A few mornings ago I read a letter in "Dear Abby." The writer declared she was fat and happy, and asked what was so wrong with that.

The woman's got guts. She's also rare. Entire industries—from liposuction clinics to women's magazines to Oprah Winfrey—have been built on the premise that most women think something is wrong with them, that there's something they should change. "Our readers want to be told what to do," I once heard a women's magazine editor say.

Sure, we can always improve. I'm not a shambling wreck, not really—but yes, I could be more organized. I could color-coordinate my wardrobe, make meals ahead of time on weekends and freeze them, buy birthday cards in advance.

But possibly . . . just possibly . . . I'm not going to change. I may never enjoy exercise that much, except for leisurely strolls. I may prefer to play with my daughter, watch a yellow-and-black spider spin her web, laugh with my husband. I may never be systematic about prayer and devotional times, as I'm told I should be. But I DO pray; I DO spend time in the Word—in my own way.

Well, we need to be saying that to each other.
Something a pastoral psychologist once wrote sticks in
my mind. "Most of us," he said, "are doing the best we
can" — given our psychological makeup, our current
circumstances, our histories. In other words, we as
Christians need to give one another the benefit of the
doubt a bit more, accept one another's (and our own)
limitations. Change what truly *needs* to be changed,
yes, but don't *assume* that someone, in the words of
my grade-school report card, "needs to improve."

None of us is able to be perfect. The Fall saw to that.

Jan, unknowingly, gave us all a special gift that day.
She did not know anyone else in the room very well,
except me — but she bestowed on us the gift of healing
honesty. And in so doing, she drew our group a little closer
and freed us to go a little deeper in showing our scars.

Last night I received a phone call from another dear
friend, someone I consider a soul-sister. She said, almost
hesitantly, "I always feel as though I call you more than
you call me." My first instinct was to think, *But I am the
woman with two heads! A busy person with places to go, people
to see!* I demurred: "Of course I call you. Anyway, who's
keeping score?" But — like Jan — she was giving me the
gift of her neediness: *I need to hear from you more. I need you.*

That, as much as anything, may be why we ought
to be showing a bit more of ourselves to each other —
to let each other see our slips hanging down below
our skirts, as it were. Like irregular puzzle pieces that
fit into a harmonious whole, we complete each other.
If we strive endlessly to present a near-perfect facade,
we are in effect saying, "I don't need you, except as an
admirer." We are also saying we don't need God.

The publisher of this book has a beautifully calli-
graphed mission statement that hangs in the company's
headquarters. I received a copy when I visited their
offices once. One evening I lay in bed examining the

symmetry of the pen strokes. *Perfect,* I thought. Then I looked more closely and realized they were not. Despite the craft of the calligrapher, each letter differed slightly.

And that was what made the lettering so beautiful: the minute flaws that showed a human hand behind the design, not a computerized typesetting machine. The subtle irregularities created a fascinating texture that drew the eye and made for something very near to art.

I worry about being perfect and tend to dwell on my various flaws. If I'm dressed to impress in a well-cut jacket and a skirt of this season's length, I'm aware that I have a hangnail on my pinkie or a loose button on my blouse. If my house is immaculate for expected company (and in my well-ordered universe there's no room for the unexpected), I stare balefully at the crack in the plaster or the coffee ring on the end table, and I flagellate myself for being so slipshod.

I need to be more like Dick, a man I met last year at a Christian convention. You couldn't miss Dick; where most of us wore suits and dresses, he stood out in his braided hair and embroidered jean jacket. I was delighted when he joined a group of us for dinner at a Chinese restaurant. As we shared Szechuan delicacies from a lazy Susan tray, Dick guided the conversation, easing our awkwardness (we didn't all know each other very well), asking everyone about their conversion experiences and sharing his own story of salvation through Jesus People U.S.A. Dick made us feel like family — accepted for who we were. For a brief few hours, I was able to forget about the upcoming awards ceremony (*Would I win? Would I receive recognition?*) and enjoy authentic Christian fellowship.

I've seen those bumper stickers that proclaim "Not Perfect, Just Forgiven." It's an accurate sentiment, but most of us don't live like we believe it.

Dick, the man with the braid, believes it and lives it—
and because he does, others are drawn to him.

My husband believes it most of the time (which is
another proof of God's great wisdom in putting us
together!). The other day I was sharing some good
news with him of a potentially exciting career opportunity. We chatted briefly about it, then started
making dinner, keeping to the schedule. He paused
and grabbed me by the shoulders. "Wait a minute!"
he said. "We're trying too hard. We should celebrate!"

Celebrate. Accept. Rejoice. Those of us who survive
by minute-to-minute planning, however necessary to oil
the gears that keep life moving, have a particular diffi-
culty with this. How can we celebrate when nothing's
defrosted for dinner and we need a haircut? What on
earth is there to rejoice about? We're screwing up!

No, we're not.

And such thinking borders on idolatry as we worship
our man-made idols of perfection, bow to our to-do lists. I
have an image of God grieving as he watches his people
scurry about like ants, striving, striving, ignoring the beauty
of his world and indicting other ants for their shortcomings.

We need each other in our incompleteness; we're
beautiful in our irregularity. This is how Dick sees;
this is how Jesus sees. And Dick does not deny flaws
and fallenness. Living in the middle of a great city,
Dick is under no illusions as to the state of the world
man has created. Yet through all that, possibly because of all that, Dick (who has stumbled through his
own valleys) chooses to affirm. To love the imperfect.

He who loses his life for my sake . . .

I'd like to try to look deeper and love the imperfections the Calligrapher has wrought in all of
us—me, you, Dick, everyone.

We just might find something very precious: we
just might find God.

21

Real Men Don't Dust

*T*he other night, I came home from work, took off
my coat, glanced at the mail (mostly those cards
that say, "Have You Seen Me?"), then went into the
kitchen.

It was spotless.

I mean, it was *immaculate*. Floor swept. Sink shiny.
Nothing on the counters except what belonged there.
For an instant, I wondered if I was in the right house.

"Fritz!" I cried in astonishment. "Look what you did!"

He smiled. "Glad you noticed. I even ran in and
wiped up the spills at the last minute."

Noticed? I was downright dazzled.

Before you start asking, "Who is this paragon
and can he be cloned?" let me tell you something:
This is totally uncharacteristic of my husband's usual
technique. To Fritz, a kitchen is "clean" if the dishes
are washed and the leftovers removed to the refrigerator. In the pans they were cooked in. With the
stirring spoon still stuck in. But to wipe the counters,
scrub the stove, or shine the sink?

I've read *The Second Shift,* the book whose premise is
that working women still assume a disproportionate

share of the chore-and-child-care load. The picture author Arlie Hochstein paints is bleak — exhausted women who have already put in a ten-hour day staying up until midnight ironing, dragging their way through the supermarket aisles, or regrouting the bathroom tiles while their husbands recline in the La-Z-Boy watching ESPN and snacking on Cheetos.

Though the book has the feel of feminist axe-grinding, statistics show Hockstein is at least partly correct. Even in households where both spouses work full time, the wife still puts in more hours of housework than her husband.

Fortunately, I don't have that problem. My husband is very good about pulling his share of the load. *My* problem is that when it comes to cleaning, his ways are not my ways.

Take, for example, the vacuuming. Maybe I'm easily entertained, but I shiver with delight when I hear that telltale rattle of sucked-up debris. Happiness for me is a new package of vacuum bags and a working brush attachment. I do baseboards, curtains, upholstery, parakeet feathers (not parakeets). Sometimes I even vacuum the coffee table ("Hello, my name is Elizabeth N., and I am compulsive.").

My husband's approach is more, uh, casual. He shuns corners and won't move things to get under them. (*It doesn't get dirty under there,* he rationalizes.) There could be a cobweb the size of a necktie hanging from the ceiling — and he would ignore it.

He thinks that if you don't *see* dirt, if it doesn't stand up and practically salute, it isn't there. I lecture him about the billions of carpet mites that hunker down in the fibers of the Stainmaster and set up housekeeping (knife and fork at the ready, as a friend of mine once said). I warn him that as we walk on the carpet, clouds of these unseen creatures are swarming through the air and getting into our breakfast cereal.

But to Fritz, the carpet isn't dirty unless it looks as if someone like "Roseanne's" John Goodman stomped through the house, leaving muddy footprints behind. Then he might say, with laserlike perception, "Boy, is this house dirty!"

There is one area in which I have relinquished control to my husband, and that is laundry. I don't do it. And although our clothes end up reasonably clean, that's *all* they are. Fritz views it as a challenge to pack the large-capacity washer as full as possible, and he never sorts lights and darks. So my daughter's once-white underwear now looks tie-dyed.

I have also tried to explain to Fritz how important it is to remove clothes from the dryer immediately after the last buzzer sounds. But with childlike trust, he actually believes that "Permanent Press" means just that. When I go to the closet in the morning to select a dress for work, I find it a mass of crinkles. "No problem," says my sanguine husband. "We'll just steam out those wrinkles in the shower!" The maddening thing is, it works.

I don't think there's a man alive who enjoys dusting, except maybe Homer Formby. Vacuuming is somehow manly and physical; you get to bang about and run a loud motor. Norman Schwarzkopf would be a great vacuumer. Even cleaning a bathroom involves the use of hazardous substances that appeal to some men's need to court danger. Dusting, however, requires fine motor skills. It seems foppish and fussy, and most men don't see its importance.

My husband hates to dust and will do it only under extreme duress (such as his wife screaming in his ear, "DUST!"). In fairness, dusting at our house is a rather complicated procedure—if you do it like I do. You see, we have collected approximately eighty-seven knickknacks that need to be *lifted up* in order to clean furniture surfaces.

Needless to say, I did not marry Homer Formby. And on the rare occasions my husband has dusted, I have discovered telltale circles of dust where he did *not* lift up all eighty-seven knickknacks. Or a coffee ring that didn't get wiped. Or something—despite my dire warnings about the host of pestiferous disease carriers that crawl out the heat ducts to take up residence on the seats of chairs *where we will be sitting*.

But I am beginning to believe that hormonal differences are stronger than C. Everett Koop-style health warnings. Real men don't dust. Period.

When it comes right down to it, it is hard to nag too much about all this. My husband doesn't just sit around watching ESPN and snacking on Cheetos. He tries to do his part around the house. And I do mine.

In the end, I have to let Fritz be Fritz. And would I really want him to change? His quirks, his eccentricities, and even his shortcomings are as endearing as the way his hair curls when it gets too long. I accepted the whole package when I got married.

Besides, I have a feeling there are barriers of gender that preclude complete success in teaching him my precepts of housework. Therefore, if I want something accomplished to my lofty standards, I will have to do it myself. Or hire someone.

Or . . . hmmm. My daughter is almost in first grade. Already she enjoys helping me clean. One Saturday we pretended to be mother and daughter servants working in a rich lady's house.

So maybe *that's* the secret. Let my husband do his macho things like cleaning out the garage, fishing the contact lenses out of the drain trap, and stomping on vicious insects. Maybe *Amanda* has a clue about sorting lights and darks. Already she does windows.

22

My Dad's Pencil Box

*They who wait for the Lord shall renew their strength,
they shall mount up with wings like eagles, they shall run
and not be weary, they shall walk and not faint.*
                                                    Isaiah 40:31 RSV

I write this now removed from both work and
home. My father, who was hospitalized for so
long, is now with the Lord, strong and whole again.
Tomorrow is Dad's memorial service. He loved
eagles, and we have selected this passage from Isaiah
as one of the Scriptures to be read.

The past few months of Dad's illness have taught
me something about patience and goodness and
mercy. In this brief interim between the initial shock
(because you are never ready for this kind of loss) and
the hubbub of tomorrow, I remember a phone conversation I just had with a colleague. He wanted to know
about the plans for the service. "We want to be there,"
he said.

I was moved by this display of kindness, and I
fought for composure. Then I gave him directions,
thanked him, and hung up. As I reflect on the things
that give me strength, on the things that renew me so

I will not be weary, I realize I need the presence of these co-workers, these brothers and sisters in Christ. Their presence tomorrow will remind me of my usual routine, will connect me with my two-headed world so that *everything* does not feel so radically changed.

Here I am now in an upstairs bedroom at my mother-in-law's, a few minutes away from the house I grew up in. My mother-in-law is in the other room showing Amanda how to use a sewing machine. I half listen to them as I mull over my life. In a few days the relatives will go home, the bustle will fade. And I will go back to work.

I will walk into that small corner office with my prized window, and my desk will be overflowing with mail and memos and telephone messages. My plant will be drooping from lack of water. My coffee cup, the one that says, "This is the day which the Lord has made," will need washing—or detoxifying. People will drop by or call to express their condolences. There will be meetings to attend, correspondence to catch up on. I will be soothed by the chirping of the phones and the clicking of the computer keys, by the half-heard laughter outside my door.

Occasionally I have walked through the corridors of my office after hours, when the building is empty and the only lights on are for security reasons. I can hear in my mind all the sounds of the workday. This building is a part of me, and as I stroll along, the sentiment that wells up within is akin to love.

This place is an anchor.

My father would understand that. He was passionate about his work. When I was young he worked in downtown Chicago; I remember him dressed in his gray suit and fedora, holding a brown leather briefcase, saying to my mother, "I'll catch the 8:11." He smelled like leather and wooden Prismacolor pencils and Beech-Nut fruit gum and shoe polish.

The colored pencils, which he kept in a dark green breadbox, were the tools of his trade; he designed furniture and jets and hospital beds. Sometimes he complained about his bosses and clients—but he was very good at his work. When he came home at night, he would call out a signature "Whoo!" to my mother, lift us up, and talk to her about his day.

All I really knew back then was that Daddy got on a puffing black train and disappeared into the big city for hours at a time. When I was a bit older, I visited his office and was impressed by the modern furniture, the glamorous secretaries, his drawing board, and his name on the office door. Once we went out to lunch at a busy downtown restaurant. The waiters seemed to know my dad—and I thought he must be very important.

I did not expect that someday *I* would be lunching and talking business in busy restaurants. Dad's work world was mostly male. Daddies went to the office and mommies stayed home. But here I am now, remembering my father and at the same time brooding about my work obligations, half-dreading, half-anticipating the mound of commitments that await me when I return.

Did my dad sometimes wish he didn't have to get up to catch the 8:11? Did he long—as I sometimes do—to sleep in? I'm not sure—Dad was an incorrigible lark who sang at the top of his lungs at dawn and thought everyone else should, too. But he may have had days when he wished he could stay home with his pretty wife and little daughters, days he wished he could putter around in the house he built on the meadows.

But he also knew that his home, in a sense, was also where his work was—where he kept that green breadbox with the Prismacolor pencils. Dad loved his work with an intensity almost equal to the passion he felt for his family.

And I understand that. Because part of *my* home is where I work, whether in my corner office in the mansard-roofed building in the suburban business park, or closeted at home with my writing.

I will be delighted to see my friends tomorrow. I will be glad for the strength-renewing routine of work. Dad, always a creature of habit, would approve.

23

November's Truth

I love November. There is something about the richness of a November sunset that makes for catch-in-the-throat beauty—all dusky violets and burnt siennas and dramatic mackerel skies now seen through branches newly bare. The layers of warmth and green are stripped away, and deep silence returns to the land.

November is majestically sad. It is hard, now, to put a good face on things, to talk of sleep and rebirth. November's song is a farewell, a losing. The grass withers, the flowers fade, and the only birds on the wing are crows. Even the sparrows fall silent. Often the sunset is hidden by freezing rain, and one is hard put to say anything lyrical about freezing rain.

Except: This, too, is God's.

There's something discomfiting about November, a reminder that life is not simple. Everything in life is not a joyful "yes," a frolicking affirmation of spring. *I create,* says the Lord; *I also bring the killing cold. I Am who I Am. Yet open your eyes and only see! For this, too, is a truth and a rigorous beauty.*

So I pause to think about stripping things to their sinew, their essence. I wrestle with myself and wonder:

Who am I once the layers come off? When I stand before God, will he say, "Well done, award-winning Christian author"? Or, "Good job, juggler of roles"?

I congratulate myself that I have done something with the tools I have been given. But November, time of truth, asks sternly: *Does any of this matter?*

Last Sunday our pastor spoke on "render unto God . . ." Everything is God's, he reminded us, yet we have to pay special attention to certain things. Among them, he said, is the human soul. And so he asked God's people, "Is it well with your soul?"

I sat listening, and, as I so often do when the sermon scratches a need, carried on an internal conversation. *Is it well with my soul? Where is my soul amid my busyness and achievements, amid my balancing act? What fruit am I yielding? Who am I trying to please?*

It happened to be Communion Sunday. So as I took the bread and the cup — behold the Lamb of God who takes away the sins of the world! — the mystery of Christ's brokenness whispered within me once again.

When I acknowledge and receive the ineffable gift, the only one that matters, I can put the other "gifts" into perspective. My writing, my commitments, my fatigue and ceaseless juggling recede into the background — just as November's sunset fades into early dark and a rising hunter's moon.

I would like to think the things I do during my days honor God. I try, in prayer, to commit my work to him. Still, I am learning anew that it is risky to cling to the wrong gods, to fall into the pharisaical trap of throwing God a bone every now and then through the correct Christian behavior. It is not enough to pray in restaurants, to recite the usual twaddle about priorities, to carry the most well-thumbed Bible to church.

The nails of the Cross go right to the bone. And when I start patting myself on the back too much, I run the risk of becoming insensate to that Cross, whose splintery roughness and ancient, hand-hewn nails I should be fingering instead.

Who I am, then, is Christ's. What that means, I am still discovering. What that costs, I shiver to contemplate. But I do know this: For me, that truth is taught by November—stern, unadorned, costly, glorious.

24

George Bailey
Was Wrong

S o, how was your Christmas?" I asked my colleague.
"Well, I was crabby and tired all day. I was up
until three the night before, wrapping presents
alone," she replied. "My husband was supposed to
assemble this big car track thing for our preschooler,
but he fell asleep and I didn't want to wake him. So
when Danny ran downstairs the next morning, he
looked under the tree and said, `Oh . . . a box.'
  "I just don't know about the `Christmas spirit.'"

  Sound familiar? This woman has two young
sons, is pregnant with her third, and works part-time.
Her husband is starting a new job and they are con-
tinuing to renovate their 125-year-old house. Maybe
she is just too busy for the much-heralded Christmas
spirit to come down the chimney into her house.
  When you work, does Christmas — in the sense of
that magical holiday glow — ever come? Or is it just
something else to be got through, a time of too many
presents to buy, cards to send (or at least think about
sending), Sunday school programs to attend?
  It wasn't this way when I was a kid growing up
in the fifties and sixties. Like all of us, I remember my

childhood Christmases. I especially remember what
my mother did—bake cookies, create handmade
decorations, take us on the train to downtown Chicago to see the Great Tree at Marshall Field's. Perhaps
the holidays were a strain for my parents (I do remember some suspicious bumps and grunts and cross
words drifting up to my bedroom around midnight
Christmas Eve, and I don't think they were from
Santa Claus). They had four children to make Christmas for, after all. But my mother was home, and I do
wonder if Christmas doesn't come more easily for
stay-at-home moms. There's something unfestive and
unfun about battling the after-work crowds at the
mall as you hunt for Baby Uh-Oh and Nintendo
Game Boy cartridges.

   We're less likely to entertain, too. One year I
decided to put on a sit-down dinner for everyone in
my department, plus spouses. I had to take a vacation
day to clean my house from top to bottom, set two
tables, buy new candles, bring out the Christmas
decorations I had not yet put up—plus make cream of
spinach soup, homemade bread, mixed green salad,
mulled cider, chicken breasts in yogurt sauce, and
fresh pears in chocolate sauce. At four I had to stop
vacuuming and start cooking, so I screamed for my
husband to take over with the Electrolux. I barely
finished my makeup when the doorbell rang.

   The dinner was delicious; the guests duly impressed. And I was exhausted.

   It's very hard for me to give up any of this, to
say, "Well, I don't have time." I enjoy maintaining the
fiction of the gracious hostess, gourmet cook,
thoughtful friend who keeps in touch across the
miles. I see those ads in Christian women's magazines
of the happy housewife penning her cards, candles
and greenery behind her. You can almost hear the

Kings College Choir caroling away in the background. I would like that to be me.

Much has been written about how we need to scale down our holiday expectations. Don't expect it to snow. Plan to fight with the relatives. Know the store will be out of the neon-green jacket your fourth-grader has been eyeing, and you will have to settle for (gasp) last year's model.

I know all that. And, as a Christian, I dismiss these things as baggage peripheral to the central meaning of the season. But beyond the desire to be the perfect hostess, to spend time baking angels and stars with my daughter, I expect that somewhere around December twentieth I will still feel the magic, still sense the coming of the Babe of Bethlehem. That amid the proverbial holiday bustle, I will hear his cries from the manger.

Christians, I think, have their own version of the movie *It's a Wonderful Life.* Remember how Jimmy Stewart, who played George Bailey, thought his life was over until a kindly guardian angel showed him how much he meant to others? By the end of the film, the Building & Loan was bailed out, George was surrounded by friends, and even his brother had come home from the war. The Christmas spirit had kicked in.

The Christian version goes something like this: Someone is lonely, too busy, feeling like a Scrooge. But then some unexpected encounter shows her Christmas is real after all. Happy ever after.

Bah, humbug!

Christmas doesn't heal. Jesus does.

Last Christmas was particularly hard for me. It was the first Christmas after my father's death. I mechanically decorated, shopped, even managed a few cards. I worked hard to ensure that Amanda, at least, would have a happy holiday. (When you're six, that means getting everything on your list.) I again took pains to explain the true meaning of the season to her. We went to *The Nutcracker*.

But I felt as if I were going through the motions. But I assumed that by Christmas Eve, that holiest of nights, I would be filled with peace and contentment.

Instead, my husband (like my friend's husband) fell asleep early. I bundled my daughter off to bed. We had about fifty presents to wrap. We did not go to church. I felt alone, sorry for myself, wondering when "it" would happen.

"It" never did. I somehow got through the festivities, primarily by forgetting about myself and concentrating on my daughter's joy. And I was glad when it was over and we could move on to the January doldrums.

A few days into January, as I finally took the toys from under the tree and pulled the cards down from the door where we had taped them, it came to me: There is a profound difference between that man-made, media-fostered creation we call "the Christmas spirit" and the presence of Christ. Christ's presence is not bound to some timetable but is available to us all year, for all time.

Oh, the Christmas spirit is real enough. It is not exactly a Santa Claus-style myth. Good feelings can warm the heart when much-missed family comes to visit, when we see an infant gazing at tree lights for the first time, when we go caroling at a nursing home.

But the warm fuzzies of the holiday alone are not enough to fill the absence of someone special to us (ask those whose sons and daughters celebrated last Christmas in the desert, in a land hostile to believers). They are not enough to ease the weariness of a tired heart.

And behind the Christmas spirit, whether or not the world acknowledges it, stands the Baby.

Maybe, then, I should not expect this day to be different from all other days, because by so doing I set myself up for disappointment. And maybe I really do need to scale back my expectations—buy store-bought decorated cookies, write notes in January, entertain potluck-style. By so doing I can . . . maybe . . . give myself more time to reflect on the coming of Christ, to listen to sacred music (not, please, the incessant jingle of "Rudolph the Red-Nosed Reindeer"), to talk to my daughter about Jesus. To be with him.

And God does meet needs in his own way, on his own perfect schedule. Looking back now, I can see how he provided throughout my time of sorrow. He brought our extended family together; we even got snow!

I have, of course, read variants of this in countless books and testimonies. I always thought it sounded nice and neat, but secretly wondered if the writer or speaker wasn't imposing a tidy framework on what essentially was a grievous circumstance.

I'm not so skeptical anymore.

The holidays are difficult enough without the added burden of sad circumstances. But it could be that if we have welcomed the Babe all year long and keep Christmas in that spirit—if we rely on Christ rather than Charles Dickens or George Bailey—the season will work its magic on us. Whether or not we find Baby Uh-Oh.

25

Pretty Pictures,
Real Lives II

S till God surprises me. Still he teaches me.
I am beginning to see that there is more than one
kind of "pretty picture" of women's lives. There are
the attractive, mostly false portraits painted by the
media both Christian and secular, the idyllic images
many of us keep trying to live up to—with decidedly
mixed results. And then there's reality.

"One thing I've been learning recently is that God
accepts me *where I am*," said a friend yesterday. "I'm
learning that he's working in me now, that I don't
have to wait until some future time when I'm perfect."

Reality, in all its imperfection, has the beauty of
truth. It's the truth of real women, seeking to live each
day with a measure of hope, humor, and grit—seeking to
live as God would have them do.

I see it in Chris, a single parent with two small
children. Chris tried for years to save her marriage,
but her husband, fighting his own demons, did not
share the same commitment. Chris has had to
struggle alone with the challenge of basic survival.
She has not had the luxury of working part time at
her job as an administrative assistant. Nor can she
afford to hire sitters, so her children are in day care.

Still, Chris is no victim. She's a confident woman
with an acerbic wit; I like being around her. She has
worked hard and smart and has earned several pro-
motions. This is her situation. She is making the best
of it. *That's* beauty.

And I see it in Virginia, who taught school part
time while rearing three children and coping with the
frequent moves demanded of a military family. Now
that her kids are all in their teens, she has resumed
work on the doctorate she left unfinished nearly two
decades ago. One of her daughters has a severe learning disability and other emotional problems. Virginia,
always ambitious, always oriented to intellectual
achievement, has learned the hard way about humility and imperfection—about patience. Yet she has
never abandoned her dream of teaching history at the
university level. God is working in Virginia, too—
right where she is.

Mary Kate hasn't known the devastation of
divorce or the anguish of caring for a child with
special needs. All she does several days a week is get
up and go to work. But it still isn't easy: as I write
this, Mary Kate is pregnant with her third child and
rises before dawn, leaving her husband and two sons
asleep, and drives her old Dodge Omni nearly an
hour to her part-time job in personnel administration.

Mary Kate has to work, but she also likes to work
and sees her job as the gateway to an eventual career
in management. She's not sure what she will do after
the baby arrives. Working is tough with small children,
let alone a newborn. Mary Kate often has shadows
under her Irish-blue eyes; her boys get sick a lot and
she worries about finances. But like most "women
with two heads," she keeps going, driven not just by
her sputtering Omni, but by her passions for her work
and her family—the two demanding gifts.

There is more beauty in these portraits of flesh-and-blood women than in a hundred magazine layouts of some executive in her vast office with a glass-topped table for a desk. There's more truth in these real lives than in a dozen saccharine treatises on the ideal Christian woman. These women don't have to live up to anything--because, with God's help, they are learning to live with authenticity — to live with two heads. And then there's me.

As I'm learning the beauty of real life, I'm also learning the truth of my own insufficiency. I tend to be a planner, a controller, a string-puller. Yet all my organizing can go only so far, and I have to yield to Another's power and comfort. And as I bump along, balancing the various demands of my life, I'm glad of his grace, which so many times has startled me out of my self-preoccupation, like a late-afternoon burst of sun through a gray overcast.

Quite without my trying to achieve it (a miracle in itself, since I'm always trying to achieve things), God's grace and mercy beam down on me, sometimes when I least expect them. A lone robin sings outside the place where my father passed away. My husband and I enjoy a tranquil morning and a great cup of coffee. A friend calls from halfway across the country and asks if I would edit her book.

These things surprise, console, encourage. My portrait is at least as full of blotches and imperfections as the others I've sketched. I, too, sometimes imagine that at some future date my closets will be organized and my correspondence answered and my husband and I will adhere to a strict schedule of evenings out.

I'm still waiting. But while I'm waiting, God is acting. *Behold, I am doing a new thing . . .*

In me. And in you.